CW01183990

TREKKING IN THE DOLOMITES

About the Author

Gillian Price was born in England but moved to Australia when young. After taking a degree in anthropology and working in adult education, she set off to travel through Asia and trek the Himalayas. The culmination of her journey was Venice where, her enthusiasm fired for mountains, the next logical step was towards the Dolomites, only hours away. Starting there, Gillian is steadily exploring the mountain ranges and flatter parts of Italy and bringing them to life for visitors in a series of outstanding guides for Cicerone.

When not out walking and taking photos with Nicola, her Venetian cartographer husband, Gillian works as a freelance travel writer and translator (www.gillianprice.eu). An adamant promoter of public transport to minimise impact in alpine areas, Gillian is also an active member of the Italian Alpine Club and the Outdoor Writers and Photographers Guild.

Other Cicerone guides by the author
Walking in the Dolomites
Walking in the Central Italian Alps
Walking in Tuscany
Walking in Sicily
Shorter Walks in the Dolomites
Walking on Corsica
Trekking in the Apennines: The Grande Escursione Appenninica
Through the Italian Alps: The Grande Traversata delle Alpi
Across the Eastern Alps: E5
Gran Paradiso: The Alta Via 2 Trek and Day Walks
Italy's Sibillini National Park: Walking and Trekking Guide
Walks and Treks in the Maritime Alps
Walking on the Amalfi Coast

TREKKING IN THE DOLOMITES
by
Gillian Price

© Gillian Price 2011
Third Edition 2011
ISBN 978 1 85284 563 6
Second Edition 2005 © Martin Collins and Gillian Price
ISBN-10 1 85284 359 4
ISBN-13 978 1 85284 359 5
First Edition 1990 © Martin Collins and Gillian Price
ISBN 978 0 90236 375 5

Printed by MCC Graphics, Spain.

A catalogue for this book is available from the British Library.
All photographs are by the author unless otherwise stated.

Dedication
For the one-and-only Nick, joke-teller and map-drawer supreme.
But he has to share this dedication with dear departed Danilo and Piero, generous souls who actively encouraged me to discover these magical mountains in my infant alpine years.

Acknowledgements
Thanks to all the walkers who wrote in with feedback and comments on the previous edition.

Advice to Readers
Readers are advised that, while every effort is made by our authors to ensure the accuracy of guidebooks as they go to print, changes can occur during the lifetime of an edition. Please check Updates on this book's page on the Cicerone website (www.cicerone.co.uk) before planning your trip. We would also advise that you check information about such things as transport, accommodation and shops locally. Even rights of way can be altered over time. We are always grateful for information about any discrepancies between a guidebook and the facts on the ground, sent by email to info@cicerone.co.uk or by post to Cicerone, 2 Police Square, Milnthorpe LA7 7PY, United Kingdom.

Front cover: On the final approach to Forcella della Roa (AV2)

CONTENTS

INTRODUCTION
The Dolomites 11
The Alta Via routes 14
Plants and flowers 16
Wildlife 18
Background reading 22
Getting there 22
Local transport 23
Information. 25
When to go 26
Accommodation. 26
Food and drink. 31
What to take. 32
Maps 33
Dos and don'ts 35
Emergencies 37
Using this guidebook 38

ALTA VIA 1 39

ALTA VIA 2 93

ALTE VIE 3–6
Alta Via 3 164
Alta Via 4 169
Alta Via 5 174
Alta Via 6 179

APPENDIX A Glossary 185

APPENDIX B Route summary tables. 187

Climbing away from Pian dei Cantoni (AV2 Stage 8)

Warning

Mountain walking can be a dangerous activity carrying a risk of personal injury or death. It should be undertaken only by those with a full understanding of the risks and with the training and experience to evaluate them. While every care and effort has been taken in the preparation of this guide, the user should be aware that conditions can be highly variable and can change quickly, materially affecting the seriousness of a mountain walk. Therefore, except for any liability which cannot be excluded by law, neither Cicerone nor the author accept liability for damage of any nature (including damage to property, personal injury or death) arising directly or indirectly from the information in this book.

To call out the Italian Mountain Rescue, ring the emergency number 118: this will connect you via any available network.

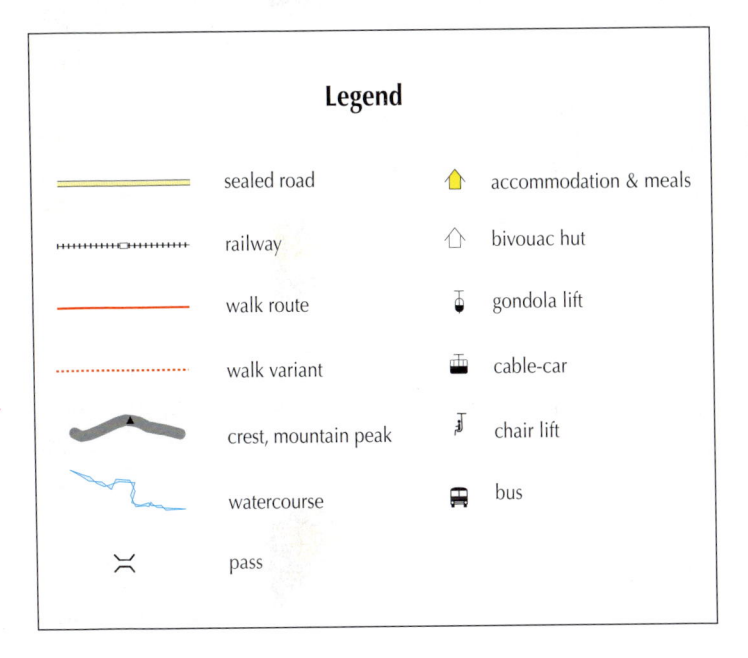

Legend

═══	sealed road	⇧	accommodation & meals
┅┅o┅┅	railway	⌂	bivouac hut
───	walk route		gondola lift
·······	walk variant		cable-car
⏜▲⏜	crest, mountain peak		chair lift
〰	watercourse	🚌	bus
✕	pass		

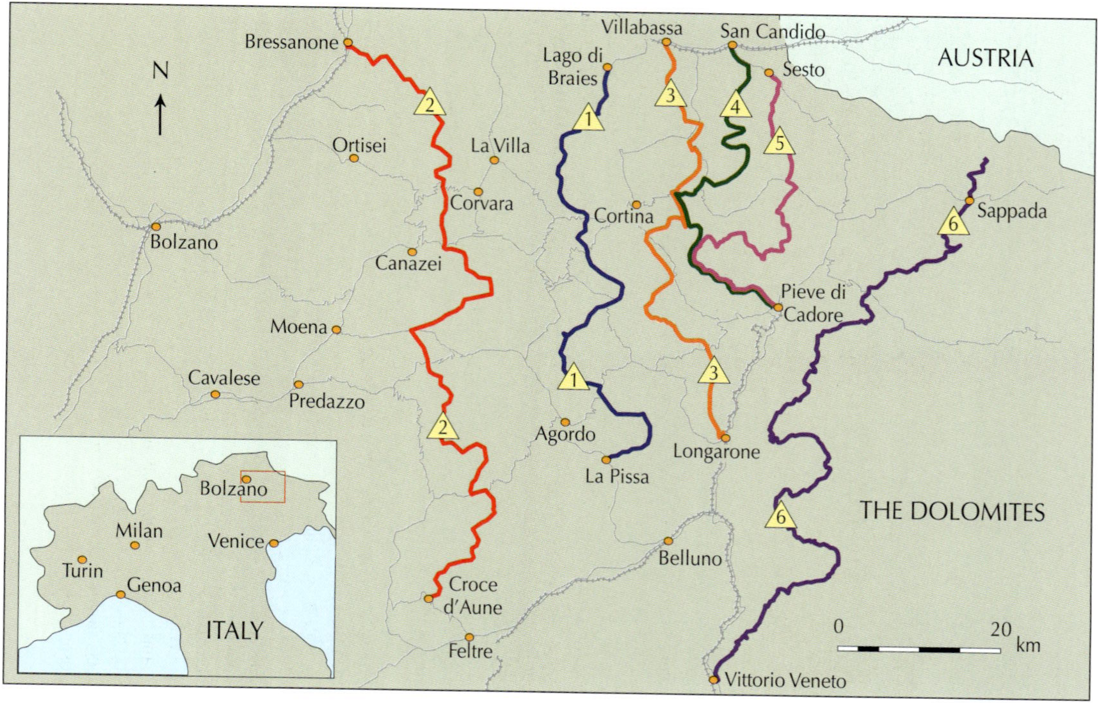
AUSTRIA
THE DOLOMITES
N
Bressanone
Villabassa
San Candido
Lago di Braies
Sesto
Ortisei
La Villa
Corvara
Cortina
Bolzano
Canazei
Sappada
Pieve di Cadore
Moena
Cavalese
Predazzo
Agordo
Longarone
La Pissa
Belluno
Croce d'Aune
Feltre
Vittorio Veneto
0
20
km
1
2
3
4
5
6
Bolzano
Milan
Venice
Turin
Genoa
ITALY

PREFACE TO THE THIRD EDITION

Vast views from Forcella Giau (AV1 Stage 5)

After a prolonged period tramping across the western Alps, it was especially exciting being back in the Dolomites and on the memorable long-distance Alta Via trails. A very first experience back in 1981 on AV1 had been both awe-inspiring and unforgettable – not least because we'd braved a storm and lashing rain equipped with little but bin liners as innovative rainskirts. It was a landmark in our lives and we joined CAI, the Italian Alpine Club, for the occasion. Since then we've been back time and time again, and barely need an excuse to jump on the train north to breathe in more of that Dolomites magnificence. The allure of these magical mountains grows with every visit – and I can also report that comfort levels in the huts have improved.

And the icing on the cake? After steadfast campaigning by concerned environmental groups such as Mountain Wilderness, the Italian Dolomites have finally been recognised as a World Heritage Site by UNESCO.

This new edition has brand new detailed route descriptions, and the main Alta Via 1 and 2 routes have been divided into manageable stages to make the treks easier to handle and organise. In addition, individual sketch maps have been drawn, while facilities and timing can be rapidly identified thanks to route profiles. Naturally, a whole host of new photos is included.

What's more, as well as the well-trodden AV1 and AV2 routes, Alta Via 3, 4, 5, and 6 are presented. Little known and even less walked, they explore wilder ranges of the Dolomites crossing valleys and settlements where tradition runs deep. Solitude and awesome beauty are the name of the game. A great boon for those seeking adventure.

Gillian Price

Towers on Peralba in the mist (AV6)

INTRODUCTION

THE DOLOMITES

What can visitors expect? This inspirational early description from John Murray in 1840 helps set the stage:

> They are unlike any other mountains, and are to be seen nowhere else among the Alps. They arrest the attention by the singularity and picturesqueness of their forms, by their sharp peaks or horns, sometimes rising up in pinnacles and obelisks, at others extending in serrated ridges, teethed like the jaw of an alligator.

Tucked up in the northeastern corner of Italy close to the border with Austria, the magnificent Dolomite mountains are a wonderland for summer walkers. Village-based resorts with facilities for all pockets are linked by good motorable roads and efficient public transport. An excellent web of marked pathways snake over mountain and vale, supported by a superb network of brilliantly located hospitable *rifugi* mountain huts that welcome walkers, feed them royally and put them up overnight. Nature lovers will be delighted by the quintessential *The Sound of Music* settings where vast expanses of sweet alpine meadows are transformed by summer into veritable seas of wild flowers. Magnificent dense evergreen and deciduous forests are widespread, as is plenty of fascinating wildlife.

Rather than a continuous alpine chain, the Dolomites consist of self-contained formations that rise to dizzy heights in soaring peaks, enthralling sculpted shapes of delicately pale rock spires and breathtaking sheer walls towering over high altitude lunar-like plateaux where people are dwarfed. In all, it is an extraordinary array of landscapes. Legend has it that the rock surface is covered in fine white gossamer, which shines splendidly in sunshine and assumes gorgeous hues of orangey-pink at sundown, a spectacular phenomenon known as 'enrosadira'. The fact is that it was woven from moon rays, an ingenious idea to help acclimatise a princess bride pining away for the lunar landscapes of her homeland...

The *Monti Pallidi* or 'Pale Mounts' as they were originally called, were renamed after French geologist Déodat de Dolomieu. Intrigued as to why they differed from other limestone ranges, he analysed their rock composition after a visit in 1788. In this analysis he discovered the principal ingredient to be calcium magnesium carbonate (later called dolomite in his honour), conspicuously unlike calcium

Lago Coldai (AV1 Stage 7)

carbonate or calcite, the more widespread type of limestone found elsewhere. Some 230 million years ago the region was covered by shallow tropical sea where marine remains and coral were gradually deposited. This progressively compressed into sedimentary rock, often with intriguing dinosaur tracks, fossilised shells and even ripple marks embedded in it. It wasn't until the 65-million-year mark that land-moving tectonic events thrust the rock dramatically upwards leading to the creation of the Alps. Recent ice ages and glacier blanketing contributed to shaping the mountains, which are subject to ongoing erosion caused by atmospheric factors wind, ice and rain – the vast scree flows are a clear example.

Due to their location, during the First World War conflict between the crumbling Austro-Hungarian Empire and fledgling Italy, the Dolomites became a war zone, with battles contesting borders that ran along high altitude mountain crests. Military mule tracks were constructed to supplement existing tracks trodden by herders and shepherds, and today they comprise a valuable part of the network of pathways. Remains of fortifications, trenches and tunnels and even the occasional rusty barbed wire and boot sole still lie scattered over mountainsides, poignant reminders of the folly that saw more troops perish under avalanches and from the terrible cold in this harsh environment than in combat.

Hostilities over, the Hapsburg Empire was dismembered, a sizeable portion going to Italy in 1919, accounting for a third of the total

THE DOLOMITES

Dolomites area. Südtirol or Alto Adige with its regional capital Bozen, or Bolzano, is dominated by German language speakers – 70 per cent of the population. During the Fascist period the inhabitants were given the terrible 'choice' of moving to allied Austria, or changing their names. Every single place name – mountains included – was translated, and schooling in Italian became compulsory. Curiously, nowadays it is the old farmer folk, educated under Mussolini's system who speak better Italian than the young people, who attend segregated parallel German- or Italian-language schools.

However, other tongues are still heard. The ancient Rhaeto-Romanic language known as Ladin (pre-dating the Latin brought by the Romans) has survived to this day and is the declared mother tongue of just over four per cent of the inhabitants. Lastly there's an intriguing linguistic pocket in the easternmost Dolomites town of Sappada where Plodarisch, an old Bavarian-Tyrolean dialect is spoken.

Adjoining the Italian-speaking Trentino region centred on Trento, the remaining southeastern chunk of the Dolomites comes under the Veneto region, long administered from Venice. Centuries ago during the glorious era of the Serenissima, immense rafts of timber harvested from the republic's carefully nurtured forests were piloted downstream to the lagoon city, essential as foundations and in shipbuilding.

The aftermath of the Second World War saw many of the Dolomite

The Pelmo appears after Forcella Giau (AV1 Stage 5)

villages dramatically impoverished and large-scale emigration overseas was common. Since then they have experienced a tourist boom encompassing winter skiing, bringing with it an improvement in life style and secure jobs, not to mention crowds, traffic and pollution. Yet the Dolomites still represent a paradise and will hopefully continue to do so with more responsible management as well as environment-conscious walkers.

THE ALTA VIA ROUTES

The Dolomites are justifiably popular. Once away from hot spots, however, adventurous visitors can easily enjoy the natural splendour all to themselves. Here lies the beauty of the long-distance, high-level trails, the *Alte Vie*, from the singular *Alta Via* (both usually abbreviated as AV) or 'high route', *Höhenweg* in German. Six established walking trails traverse the Dolomites from top to bottom, north to south, maintaining medium-high altitude and exploring spectacular angles of the different mountainous groups – from Lagazuoi to Sella, Pale di San Martino to Puez-Odle, Sesto to the Marmarole, to mention but a handful and begin the important process of name familiarisation. On any one of the routes walkers can expect to see up to 80 per cent of all the Dolomites!

The *Alte Vie* vary in length from 6 to 13 days, and range from easy ambles to difficult aided climbs. Overnight stops are made at manned mountain huts and/or guesthouses so on the whole walkers can travel light. AV3–6 use bivouac huts as well. Naturally, self-sufficient trekkers can camp out, giving great flexibility and freedom. The two main routes, AV1 and AV2, are both well walked and clear to follow and are described in detail in this guidebook.

A great dilemma is which Alta Via to choose, as they differ quite dramatically. Beginners need go no further than AV1. Spread over 11 days and 120km, with a highest point of 2752m, it is straightforward yet astoundingly rewarding, and perfectly suited for a first alpine experience. It visits the Fanes area, Lagazuoi and many Cortina mountains, Pelmo, Civetta, Moiazza and the Dolomiti Bellunesi. A decent choice of dormitory accommodation or guesthouses is available, for softer options. In terms of overall difficulty it rates Grade 2 (see below) with the exception of a single short section in Stage 5, avoidable thanks to a variant. On the other hand experienced walkers will enjoy lengthening Stage 6 by breaking off to traverse the breathtaking Pelmo. The final stage can also be varied thanks to a via ferrata (aided climb) variant.

Note AV1 has become popular with organised groups, so individual walkers are advised to book accommodation well ahead.

Naturally AV2 is the perfect 'second' Dolomites trek! Dubbed the 'Alta

THE ALTA VIA ROUTES

At Forca Rossa (AV2 Stage 6)

Via delle Leggende', it is longer and undeniably more strenuous than AV1, and remains higher for longer. Over 13 days 160km are covered, the route straying as high as 2900m in severe environments. Numerous aided and exposed sections are encountered, although several can be detoured. It rates a challenging Grade 3 'at worst'.

AV2 traverses Plose, Puez-Odle, Sella, Pale di San Martino and the Alpi Feltrine and uses a choice of huts and the occasional hotel.

Note The climber's variant across the Marmolada and its glacier is not described here, as it requires both experience and specific gear.

En route numerous detours to villages and towns for shops or emergencies are possible, but they devour precious holiday time. These can also serve as alternative ways to enter the Alte Vie. All are explained at the appropriate point in walk descriptions.

Typical waymarking for these first routes is '1' or '2' in a blue or red triangle, but this is often faded or missing and rarely encountered, so local path numbers need to be followed on many stretches.

Of a more demanding flavour, the remaining four AV – 3, 4, 5 and 6 – are presented in summary form giving the flavour and difficulty of the itinerary accompanied by instructive diagram maps showing facilities and transport. (The additional routes AV7 and AV8 have not been included as they are quite short.)

They make their way across a combination of well trodden and wilder mountain chains and on the whole see fewer walkers. By and large these are for trekkers with a little climbing experience who are prepared to carry their own food, sleeping and cooking gear, as several nights are spent in bivouac huts. Notwithstanding, the average walker will find straightforward village-to-village or hut-to-hut chunks are easily detached. A host of variants exist, not all covered in this guide.

Generally speaking, thanks to the web of marked pathways, refuges and capillary public transport in the Dolomites, anyone can concoct their own customised itinerary to fit in with holiday dictates and personal needs. A host of further suggestions for multi-day as well as single day walks can be found in the Cicerone guides *Walking in the Dolomites* and *Shorter Walks in the Dolomites*.

PLANTS AND FLOWERS

July is the best month for Alpine flowers, but August isn't bad either on the rocky uplands once the last traces of snow have melted. However, September and October also have their surprises.

The Dolomites boast 1500 species of glorious flowering plants, a quarter of the total found in Italy. It's impossible not to be impressed by the amazing spreads. Heading the list in terms of popularity is the edelweiss of *The Sound of Music* fame. While not spectacular, it has creamy felty petals in a star formation and grows either prostrate or upright on stony terrain. The flower is said to have been brought from the moon for a legendary princess, a memory of the pale lunar landscape to which she was accustomed.

Trumpet gentians

In dramatic colour contrast are the deep blue trumpet gentians that burst through the grass, demanding admiration. Meadows harbour striking orange lilies and the wine-red martagon variety, which vie with each other for brilliance. Light woodland and slopes are colonised by spreads of alpenrose, a type of rhododendron that has masses of pretty red-pink flowers.

PLANTS AND FLOWERS

Edelweiss

Moretti's bellflower

Orange lily

King of the Alps

Rhaetian poppies

Pasque flowers

Round-leaved pennycress

One of the earliest blooms to appear is the Alpine snowbell, its fragile fringed blue-lilac bells even sprout in snow patches thanks to an 'antifreeze' carbohydrate they possess. Never far away are delicate pasque flowers in white or yellow.

Shaded clearings are the places to look for the unusual lady's slipper orchid, recognisable for a sizeable yellow lip receptacle crowned by maroon petals, while elongated purple or tiny black vanilla orchids are common on rich pasture. Perfumed Rhaetian poppies brighten bleached scree slopes with patches of yellow and orange, companions to clumps of pink thrift or round-leaved

17

TREKKING IN THE DOLOMITES

pennycress, which is honey-scented. Another rock coloniser is saxifrage, literally 'rock breaker' for its deep-reaching roots.

A rare treat is the devil's claw, which specialises in hanging off vertical rock faces. A member of the rampion family, it sports a segmented pointy lilac flower with curly stigma. Another precious bloom is the king of the Alps, a striking cushion of pretty blue, almost a dwarf version of forget-me-not. Moretti's bellflower – with rounded deep blue petals, nestling in high crevices – is an endemic that grows in abundance in the southern Dolomites. Dry sun-scorched terrain is preferred by curious houseleeks, which bear an uncanny resemblance to miniature triffids.

As far as trees go, over 1000m is the realm of conifers such as silver fir along with 'high achievers' arolla pine and larch, which can reach 2600m altitudes. A great coloniser of high altitude scree is the dwarf mountain pine, whose springy branches invade paths. Remarkable 'bonsai' trees include net-leaved willow, whose closely packed root system creeps over rock surfaces.

WILDLIFE

It seems a miracle that wild animals still call the European Alps home. Not only do the creatures have to adapt to the harsh environment and climate, but they also have to deal with ongoing threats from mankind such as roads, ski resorts and hunting. However, a handful of protected areas have been established across the Dolomites.

The easiest animals to see when you're out walking are marmots. These adorable furry creatures look a bit like beavers (without the flat tail) and live in extensive underground colonies. Wary of foxes and eagles who can carry off their young, they always have a sentry posted, an older animal who utters heart-stopping warning whistles to summon the tribe back home. Marmots hibernate from October to April, waking but once a month to urinate. Now protected, they were once hunted for their skins and fat, and paraded in streets fairs.

Conifer woods are home to 'bambi' roe deer and rarer red deer. Higher up, impossibly steep rock faces and scree slopes are the ideal terrain for herds of fleet-footed chamois, mountain goats with short hooked horns and light brown coats. More impressive are the stocky ibex sporting thicker grooved horns. They were re-introduced to the Dolomites 40 years ago from the Valle d'Aosta where a single group survived in a royal game reserve. Well-established groups are easily observed on the Croda del Becco, Sella and the Marmolada.

Brown bears were hunted to near extinction in the 1800s; just a tiny below-survival-threshold nucleus hung on in the Brenta Dolomites. However, sightings of plucky souls venturing over from neighbouring

WILDLIFE

Marmot

Chamois

Torre Venezia dominates the route to Rifugio Vazzoler (AV1 Stage 7)

WILDLIFE

Slovenia are becoming more common. A bear was actually photographed in Val Canali in the Pale di San Martino in June 2009.

Birdwatchers will enjoy the small delightful songsters in woods, although sizeable birds of prey such as kites, buzzards and golden eagles may be spotted above the tree line.

A special treat is the showy high altitude wallcreeper, a bit like a woodpecker. Fluttering over extraordinarily sheer rock faces in its hunt for insects, it flashes its black plumage with red panels and white dots, attracting attention with its shrill piping call.

Back at ground level are salamanders. Unlike lizards, which sunbathe in dry places, salamanders are unhurried prehistoric-looking creatures found on grass and stony terrain in wet weather. They come in shiny black and a spectacular gold-patched version known as the fire salamander, reputed in ancient times to be able to pass through flames without coming to harm.

Two creatures that you may encounter are potentially – but not necessarily – dangerous.

Snakes are not uncommon. However, only the viper (adder) is venomous. Tawny brown with a diamond-shaped head and distinctive zigzag markings down its back, it grows up to 70cm in length. Vipers are commonly encountered on open terrain in the vicinity of old herders' huts where they hunt small rodents, especially in the southern Dolomites. They sun themselves to raise body temperature so may seem sluggish if disturbed, reacting with a threatening hiss in self-defence. Step back and give them time to slither away to safety. Should you be bitten, waste no time calling for help and in the meantime immobilise the bite area with a bandage. If possible stay put. Attacks are rarely fatal but it's best to get expert medical assistance as quickly as possible.

The second 'warning' regards ticks or *zecche*, some of which carry Lyme's disease and even TBE (Tick-Borne Encephalitis), life-threatening for humans. The problem concerns the Feltre and Belluno districts crossed during the concluding stages of AV1 and AV2, and applies to heavily wooded areas with thick undergrowth. Sensible precautions include wearing long light-coloured trousers which show up the tiny black pinpoints more easily, and not sitting in long grass. Inspect your body and clothes carefully after a walk for any suspect black spots or undue itching, a sign of a tick that may have attached itself to you. However, before attempting removal by grasping head and body with tweezers, take the time (5min) to suffocate it by applying a cream such as toothpaste or oil so it loosens its grip. It's a good idea to go to the nearest hospital, where an antibiotic may be prescribed as a precaution.

Trekking in the Dolomites

BACKGROUND READING

Plenty of inspirational travel accounts from the mid 1800s and early 1900s are available in libraries and on the web and make for delicious reading. John Murray's *Handbook for travellers in Southern Germany* with its enthralling descriptions of the Dolomites was a pioneering work from 1840. Later came the ground-breaking travel log *The Dolomite Mountains: Excursions through Tyrol, Carinthia, Carniola, and Friuli* by Josiah Gilbert and GC Churchill (1864). One of the best reads is Amelia Edwards' 1873 *Untrodden Peaks and Unfrequented Valleys: A Midsummer Ramble in the Dolomites*. Hard on its heels came renowned mountaineer DW Freshfield's *Italian Alps: Sketches in the Mountains of Ticino, Lombardy, the Trentino, and Venetia* in 1875, especially poetic. Of great interest for flower hunters is *The Dolomites* by Reginald Farrer (1913).

GETTING THERE

The Dolomites are located in the northeast of Italy, not far from the border with Austria, and all the Alte Vie begin on the northernmost edge.

A logical approach from northern Europe and the UK is by rail via Munich, Innsbruck then the Brenner Pass. Eurail passes for the under-26-year-olds make this an especially attractive option, a leisurely and less polluting option than flying. A similar route can be followed by car.

For AV1 you need to change trains at Fortezza for the Val Pusteria branch line E past Brunico. The most convenient railway station is Villabassa, which has SAD buses to the route start at Lago di Braies (also known by its German name Pragser Wildsee). Drivers will find the turn-off for Lago di Braies halfway between Monguelfo and Villabassa.

For AV2, from the Brenner Pass continue S the short distance to Bressanone and the trailhead.

However, most walkers will be flying in. Convenient airports include Venice's Marco Polo (www.veniceairport.com) or Treviso (www.trevisoairport.it), 36km inland. Take a bus from either to Mestre railway station for a train to Verona thence the line N via Bolzano. Bressanone is where you get off for the AV2, whereas those heading for AV1 need to proceed to Fortezza, and change for Villabassa as above.

For a more scenic route with similar timing, take the ATVO (www.atvo.it) coach from Venice's Piazzale Roma bus terminal via Mestre railway station and Treviso bus station, destination Cortina. Here, change to a SAD bus to Dobbiaco to pick up the Lago di Braies run.

A further variant entails the train from Mestre via Treviso to Calalzo, where you transfer to a Dolomiti Bus to Cortina, continuing as above.

LOCAL TRANSPORT

The public transport network in the Dolomites is extensive, reliable and very reasonably priced. What's more it means people can visit these magical mountains without contributing unnecessarily to air pollution and traffic congestion.

The Italian railways can be contacted for timetables and information at ☎ 892021 or www.trenitalia.com. Useful lines are Verona–Bolzano–Bressanone–Fortezza then the branch line Fortezza–San Candido (which continues to Lienz in Austria), otherwise Venice–Mestre–Treviso–Calalzo.

For buses, summer timetables generally correspond to Italian school holidays, mid-June to mid-September. The exact dates vary year to year, company to company and can be checked on the relevant web sites – see below. For instance SAD in Südtirol usually extend services through to October.

The Südtirol valleys are the responsibility of SAD ☎ 840 000471 www.sii.bz.it. Buy tickets on board. If you have a small group or plan on making multiple journeys it's worth asking for a €10 *carta valori*, which is valid for one year.

The Trentino region is covered by Trentino Trasporti (also known as Atesina) ☎ 0461 821000 www.ttesercizio.it (click on *orari*). Fares are purchased at bus terminals or on board for minor stops.

The main bus company in the Veneto covering the Belluno and Cortina districts is Dolomiti Bus ☎ 0437 941167 www.dolomitibus.it. Tickets should be purchased before boarding at newsagents or cafés

Boarding the bus at the conclusion of AV1 (AV1 Stage 11)

At Casera Pioda and a view to the Pelmo (AV1 Stage 6)

displaying the appropriate logo, otherwise the driver will add a modest surcharge.

Parts of the easternmost Dolomites such as Sappada in the Friuli-Veneto border region are served by SAF buses ☎ 800 915303 www.saf.ud.it. The Cimolais–Erto–Longarone line is by ATAP ☎ 800 101040 www.atap.pn.it. Pay on boarding.

A taxi can always be summoned by asking at the local café/bar.

INFORMATION

The Italian Tourist Board has offices all over the world and can help intending travellers with general information: UK www.enit.it, 1 Princes St, London W1B 2AY ☎ 0207 3993562; Australia www.italiantourism.com.au, Level 4, 46 Market St, Sydney ☎ 02 92621666; US www.italiantourism.com 630, Fifth Avenue Suite 1565, New York, NY 10111 ☎ (212) 2455618.

A list of local information offices useful for the Alte Vie follows. They are indicated by ⓘ in route descriptions:

Agordo ☎ 0437 62105
Arabba ☎ 0436 79130
Auronzo ☎ 0435 9359
Belluno ☎ 0437 940083
Cortina d'Ampezzo
☎ 0436 3231/2/3
Falcade ☎ 0437 599241
Feltre ☎ 0439 2540
Forno di Zoldo ☎ 0437 787349
Misurina ☎ 0435 39016

Pieve di Cadore ☎ 0435 31644
Rocca Pietore ☎ 0437 721319
San Vito di Cadore ☎ 0436 9119
Sappada ☎ 0435 469131
Zoldo Alto ☎ 0437 789145
www.infodolomiti.it or
www.dolomiti.org

Dobbiaco ☎ 0474 972132
San Candido ☎ 0474 913149
Sesto ☎ 0474 710310
Villabassa ☎ 0474 745136
www.hochpustertal.info/it

Bressanone ☎ 0472 836401
San Andrea ☎ 0472 850008
www.brixen.org

Fiera di Primiero ☎ 0439 62407
San Martino di Castrozza
☎ 0439 768867
www.sanmartino.com

Longarone ☎ 0437 770177
www.prolocolongarone.it
Moena ☎ 0462 609770
www.fassa.com
San Vigilio di Marebbe
☎ 0474 501037
www.sanvigilio.org
Santa Cristina ☎ 0471 777800
www.valgardena.it
Vittorio Veneto ☎ 0438 57243
http://tourism.provincia.treviso.it

The parks on the Alte Vie are:

- Parco Naturale delle Dolomiti d'Ampezzo www.dolomitiparco.com

TREKKING IN THE DOLOMITES

- Parco Naturale Fanes-Senes-Braies, Puez-Odle and Dolomiti di Sesto www.provincia.bz.it/natura
- Parco Naturale Paneveggio Pale di San Martino www.parcopan.org
- Parco Nazionale delle Dolomiti Bellunesi www.dolomitipark.it.

Further Alta Via information can be found on www.dolomiti-altevie.it, but it is rarely updated.

WHEN TO GO

The answer is European summer, starting from mid-June when the huts open. This usually corresponds to a period when the last of the winter snow has melted off the paths, making for straightforward walking. July can be marvellous. However – and this is a big however – the situation varies wildly. To be on the safe side, if you're a beginner, you may be happier visiting in August. While this will mean busier paths and accommodation, rest assured that path conditions will be more favourable. Generally speaking, Italian alpine summers mean sunshine and heat, relieved by rain storms that build up during the day. While short and sweet, they may feature thunder and lightning.

September to October is the tail part of the Dolomites season and usually translates into crystal clear skies, none of that summer humidity and haze, and quieter paths as fewer people are around; in short, perfect conditions. The downside is the vegetation, as the intense alpine green will have faded, but yellows and pre-autumn shades will be beginning. The chance of an odd storm and possibly a flurry or two of snow on high reaches are also on the cards. Lastly, you'll need to check that huts are still operating. Generally speaking those in the northern Dolomites (the Südtirol region) tend to stay open longer (through to October) than those in the southern districts, which shut in late September.

ACCOMMODATION

Rifugi

For the most part *rifugi* (*Hütten* in German) are used. These are hostel-like structures built in amazing high altitude spots mostly far from motorable roads and towns, and reachable exclusively on foot. Along with a number of privately owned chalets, most were the work of far-seeing pioneer members of the Italian and Austrian-German Alpine Clubs (respectively CAI and DÖAV) back in the late 1800s when Dolomites mountaineering was in its heyday. Thankfully somewhat modernised since, they provide walkers and climbers with excellent home-cooked hot meals and drinks and overnight accommodation throughout the summer months as well as a limited winter season too in some cases. A *custode*, or guardian, often a qualified alpine guide, is in permanent residence with family

ACCOMMODATION

Typical refuge dormitory (Rifugio Pramperet, AV1 Stage 9)

Sassolungo from Passo Gardena (AV2 Stage 4)

members and assorted staff. Someone is always on duty to welcome guests, deal with emergencies and satisfy needs – within reason.

Anybody is welcome to stay in the refuges; membership is not compulsory. Sleeping quarters usually consist of a *dormitorio* (also called a *camerone*) catering for up to 20 people. This will be fitted with bunk beds, pillows and blankets, but guests must have their own sleeping sheet – on sale in many huts. Smaller rooms are often available if you desire privacy – request a *camera*. Unless *con bagno* (with en suite) is specified, a very rare occurrence, bathrooms are shared and guests need their own towels. Water is scarce in the Dolomites due to the dolomite-limestone rock (most surface water disappears underground) as well as the dearth of glaciers and permanent snowfields. The bottom line is – don't always expect a shower. Where available, they come at a price and a token is needed – be warned that showers may be timed so be quick if you don't want to end up in a lather that you can't rinse off! For the purposes of this guidebook, it is safe to assume there is a hot shower unless specified otherwise in the route description.

More importantly the water may occasionally not be drinkable – denoted in Italian as *acqua non potabile*, *Kein Trinkwasser* in German. It may be devoid of salts if it comes from snow or ice or rock run-off, and unsuitable for human consumption; this is the case in all the refuges

ACCOMMODATION

in the Pale di San Martino on AV2. Especially low temperature may also be the cause. Very rarely is it a case of bacterial contamination due to the presence of livestock. In any case check with the hut guardian and drink at your own risk. Safe bottled water is always on sale.

Rates differ according to which category a hut belongs to, related to ease of access and distance from roads. Generally speaking members (*soci*) of CAI and affiliated clubs can count on spending around €40 for *mezza pensione*/half board (3-course dinner, overnight stay, breakfast) and a drink or two. Non-members (*non soci*) should allow €10 more. Naturally some saving can be made if you opt out of *mezza pensione* and fill up on pasta, supplementing it with your own food. Overnight stay in Italian is *pernottamento*. Meals can be ordered individually if you don't go all-inclusive, but it's often a good deal.

Membership of CAI (Club Alpino Italiano) is open to non-Italians. Intending members need to apply to individual branches; the complete list can be found at www.cai.it. Annual fees vary from branch to branch. They tend to be around €40, with reduced rates for additional family members. Residents of Great Britain may find it easier to join the UK branch of the Austrian Alpine Club www.aacuk.org.uk ☎ 01707 386740 or the British Mountaineering Council www.thebmc.co.uk ☎ 0870 0104878, but the BMC charge extra for reciprocal rights.

Carry a good supply of euros in cash and where possible settle your bill in the evening to save wasting precious time in the morning. Some huts now accept credit card payments but check individual hut entries and never take it for granted.

Advance booking is now often possible online as many huts have web sites – see individual entries – but a confirmation email is recommended.

Note Be aware that few huts actually have internet access so emails can only be accepted outside the opening period.

Reservation is essential for mid-summer weekends, and recommended for the AV1 in general. That said, many walkers go one day at a time, phoning ahead from hut to hut. This is viable if you're versatile as many alternatives are listed. Staff will always phone ahead if you don't feel up to it.

If phoning or faxing from abroad use the Italian country code +39 and do not remove the initial 0 when dialling the number. All of the refuges and hotels have a phone, occasionally only a mobile – recognisable by a number starting with 3.

Most CAI huts have a *ricovero invernale*, a basic winter room for emergencies when the refuge itself is closed.

Both the main Alta Via routes touch on villages and road passes with hotels for those with sufficient funds who feel the need to treat themselves. These are listed in the walk description at the relevant points. *Gasthof* is German for guesthouse, and Italian variants include *albergo*, *locanda* and *pensione*.

Bivouac Huts

A *bivacco* in Italian is a handy unmanned structure, usually a basic metal cabin or a converted shepherds' or woodcutters' hut fitted out by a local CAI branch. Unless specified otherwise, they are always open and can be used by anyone. Facilities range wildly; all have bunk beds but not necessarily mattresses. Blankets, stove and utensils are variables so intending users should carry a sleeping bag, food and some sort of cooker. If no water is on hand, there will usually be an arrow or sign for *acqua* (water) or *sorgente* (spring) pointing to the nearest source. Bivouac huts can be life-savers in bad weather or emergencies, so users should always make sure the place is left in good condition and closed up, and any supplies replenished. Several in key spots come in handy for independent trekkers on the AV2. However, for AV3–6 they are essential in the absence of manned *rifugi*.

Camping

If you're prepared to carry the extra weight of tent, sleeping bag and cooking gear along with supplementary water and food, then wild camping can make these long-distance routes pure magic. However – and this is a big 'however' – these are not strolls, and walkers need to be fit and sufficiently experienced for testing long ascents and descents in alpine environments shouldering a cumbersome rucksack.

Another big 'however' concerns the park areas traversed. Single overnight pitches are only tolerated in the realms of Pale di San Martino Park on AV2, at a reasonable distance from a structure such as a refuge. In all the other protected areas it's forbidden and backpackers risk fines. To camp in the vicinity of any hut outside the parks it's best to enquire of the staff first; if allowed, they'll usually suggest a good spot. Naturally you can partake of meals in the premises. In general on medium-altitude terrain finding wild pitches is not a great problem, as long as you stay away from farms and livestock for your own safety. Wherever you camp be discreet and leave no traces.

Replenishing food supplies is not an easy task on the AV and requires time-consuming detours: a glance at the maps shows where roads are crossed and the route description gives public transport to grocery shops. There are no shops on the AV1 but you should be able to catch buses from Rifugio Pederü (Stage 2), Passo Falzarego (Stage 4) and Passo Staulanza (Stage 6). During AV2 groceries can be replenished at Malga Ciapela (Stage 6) without making a diversion.

FOOD AND DRINK

Meals are important in the day of a walker. *Colazione* or breakfast is generally continental style, with *caffè latte* (milk coffee) or *tè* (tea) to accompany bread, butter and jam. Refuge staff are always happy to prepare rolls (*panini*) if you need a picnic lunch but it's best to get your order in the evening before.

Dinner usually means a choice of a first course (*primo piatto*), namely *minestrone* vegetable soup or pasta with a meat (*ragù*) or tomato sauce *al pomodoro*. If you're lucky you'll be offered specialities such as *gnocchi di patate con ricotta affumicata*, which is a serving of tiny delicate potato dumplings with smoked cheese. *Canederli* or savoury bread dumplings flavoured with speck (smoked ham) and chives and served in consommé or with melted butter, hail from the Südtirol. *Casunziei* is tender ravioli with a beetroot filling, served with butter and poppy seeds.

The second course will be a serving of meat: *manzo* is beef, *maiale* pork, and *vitello* veal. *Tagliata* is a type of steak while *Pastin* is a flavoursome peppery sausage from the Belluno region. A curious offering is a fresh local cheese that is grilled or pan-fried in butter and cream, and known as *Tosèla* around Fiera di Primiero or *Schiz* in the southern Belluno district.

Polenta is common, thick steaming hot cornmeal served with spicy meat stew goulash, *funghi* (wild mushrooms) or *formaggio fuso* (melted cheese). A good filler.

Frutti di bosco are wild berries, served on cakes or with ice cream. One highly recommended popular

Dinner time at last! (Rifugio Pramperet, AV1 Stage 9)

TREKKING IN THE DOLOMITES

Tyrol dessert is *Kaiserschmarrn*, a pancake with dried fruit and liberally spread with jam, a meal in itself. A speciality of the northernmost Ladin valleys of the Dolomites is *Zelten*, a rich biscuit-like concoction made with dried fruit that travels well in rucksacks. Other desserts will be home-made *crostata* fruit tart or *Apfelstrudel*, a luscious thin pastry case filled with sliced apple and spices.

Wine and beer are on offer as well as soft drinks.

Note Unless you plan on resting the following day, beware the lethal *grappas* home-brewed by many mountain dwellers. Flavoured with bilberries, sultanas, pine resin and unbelievably bitter gentian root, dark bottles with unidentified floating things are often offered to unsuspecting foreigners as a genuine gesture of hospitality. Be warned!

WHAT TO TAKE

The bottom line is – much less than you think! Basic items for personal comfort and gear to cover all weather extremes are essential, but be strict with yourself and remember you'll have to lug your stuff over the mountains for days on end. Then there's the safety factor: an overly heavy rucksack can become a hazard, putting walkers off-balance and leading to unpleasant falls and serious accidents.

Really need to take that paperback? The 10pm 'lights out' rule in huts precludes bedtime reading, and communal meal times can be profitable for trying out your language skills with Italian and German walkers.

The following check list will help newcomers:

- comfortable boots with ankle support and non-slip Vibram-type sole; preferably not brand new
- rucksack – 35-litre capacity should do; plastic or stuff bags for separating contents
- light footwear such as sandals for evenings
- whistle, small headlamp or torch with spare batteries for calling for help and exploring wartime tunnels
- lightweight sleeping sheet
- towel and personal toiletries (preferably small quantities) in plastic containers
- high energy snack food such as muesli bars
- maps, altimeter, compass and binoculars
- supply of euros and credit card
- telescopic trekking poles to help wonky knees on steep descents
- sunglasses, hat, chapstick and high factor cream. For every 1000m you climb the intensity of the sun's UV rays increases by 10 per cent, augmented by reflection on snow. This, combined with lower levels of humidity and pollution which act as filters in other places, means you need a cream with a much higher protection factor than at sea level.

- alpine club membership card
- water container – plastic mineral water bottles are perfect
- mobile phone, charger with adaptor
- foam ear plugs – they occupy next to no space and ensure a good night's sleep in a dormitory crowded with snorers
- first aid kit and essential medicines
- layers of clothing for dealing with everything from scorching sun to a snow storm: t-shirts and shorts, comfortable long trousers (not jeans), warm fleece, a woolly hat and gloves (which can come in handy when used to protect your hands on cabled stretches)
- waterproofs – jacket, over-trousers and rucksack cover; a fold-up umbrella is a godsend for people who use spectacles
- Both AV1 and AV2 have aided stretches of varying lengths and difficulty, and a waist rope and karabiner clips can be reassuring without the bulk of the full via ferrata set, although be aware that these do not spell total protection and safety.

The variant at the end of AV1 along with long chunks of AV4, AV5 and AV6 are full-blooded via ferrata routes and require the appropriate experience and, or, a qualified guide as well as the following gear:

- helmet – for protection against falling stones. Make sure it conforms to UIAA (Union Internationale des Associations d'Alpinisme) standards, and remember: it's only effective if it's strapped to your head and not in your rucksack.
- full body harness and self-belay set. This comprises belay ropes, karabiners and a KISA (Kinetic Impact Shock Absorber). The more recent Y-type is UIAA approved.

For more detail consult *Via Ferratas of the Italian Dolomites: Vol 1* and *Vol 2*, both published by Cicerone Press.

MAPS

The sketch maps included in this guide help in general orientation and pre-trip preparation; they give route location and information about important landmarks and geographical features. However, they are no substitute for a detailed commercial map.

The Tabacco 1:25,000 *carta topografica per escursionisti* are by far the best walking maps for the Dolomites. They can be consulted but unfortunately not ordered at www.tabaccoeditrice.com. All are sold throughout the Dolomites and leading booksellers in the UK such as the Map Shop www.themapshop.co.uk or Stanfords www.stanfords.co.uk if you prefer to purchase them beforehand.

They use a continuous red line for a wide track, while a broken red line indicates a marked path of average

Viel del Pan and the Marmolada (AV2 Stage 5)

difficulty. Red dots denote routes that are exposed or less clear and crosses show aided sections such as cable or ladders and via ferrata routes.

With slight overlaps, the following sheets are needed:

- **Alta Via 1:** 031 'Dolomiti di Braies' for Stages 1–2; 03 'Cortina d'Ampezzo e Dolomiti Ampezzane' for Stages 2–4 and 1st part of Stage 5; 025 'Dolomiti di Zoldo, Cadorine e Agordine' for Stages 5 (2nd part) to 11.
- **Alta Via 2:** 030 'Bressanone/ Brixen Val di Funes/Villnöss' for Stages 1–3; 07 'Alta Badia-Arabba-Marmolada' for Stages 3–5; 015 'Marmolada-Pelmo-Civetta-Moiazza' for Stages 6–7; 022 'Pale di San Martino' for Stages 8–12; 023 'Alpi Feltrine-Le Vette-Cimònega' for Stages 12–13.

The Kompass 1:50,000 'Wanderkarte' series is also useful, but their graphic work is not as clear. For AV1, sheets 57, 55 and 77; for AV2, sheets 56, 59 and 76.

The relevant Tabacco 1:25,000 maps for the remaining Alte Vie are:

- **AV3:** sheets 031, 03, 025
- **AV4:** sheets 010, 03, 016
- **AV5:** sheets 010, 017, 016
- **AV6:** sheets 01, 02, 021, 012, 024

The glossary in Appendix A contains terminology found on maps.

Note In view of the area's history (see 'The Dolomites' above) both Italian, German and local Ladin versions of names are used on maps, with myriad spellings. Be prepared for discrepancies between different map editions and signposts, as changes are ongoing. One to watch out for is the term *rifugio*, transformed into *Ücia* in Ladin. For the purposes of this guide the Italian names have been given preference to avoid weighing the text down; however, the German or Ladin are sometimes used where they differ dramatically. As if that wasn't enough, dialect place names are creeping back into use in the Veneto as well with examples such as 'Zita' to replace 'Città'.

Waymarking in this part of Italy consists of red/white bars painted on prominent landmarks such as outcrops or trees, as well as signposts. An identifying path number is usually included. An Alta Via route is generally denoted by a triangle bearing the relevant number.

DOS AND DON'TS

It's better to arrive early and dry, than late and wet.
Maxim for long-distance walkers

- Find time to get in good shape before setting out on your holiday, as it will maximise enjoyment. The wonderful scenery will be better appreciated in the absence of exhaustion, and healthy walkers will react better in an emergency.
- Don't be overly ambitious; choose itineraries suited to your capacity. Read the walk description before setting out.
- Don't set out late on walks and always have extra time up your sleeve to allow for detours due to collapsed bridges, wrong turns and missing signposts. Plan on getting to your destination at an early hour in hot weather, as afternoon storms are not uncommon.
- Stick with your companions and don't lose sight of them. Remember that the progress of groups matches that of the slowest member.
- Avoid walking in brand new footwear to avoid blisters; leave those worn-out boots in the shed, as they may prove unsafe on slippery terrain. Choose your footwear carefully!
- Don't overload your rucksack. Weigh it on the bathroom scales – 10kg absolute maximum! 5kg is achieveable. Remember that drinking water and food mean extra weight. Finally, bear in mind that as the afternoon wears on and that hut seems ever further away, your pack will inexplicably get heavier.
- Check the weather forecast if possible – Tourist Offices and hut guardians are in the know. For the Südtirol see www.suedtirol.info, Trentino has www.meteotrentino.it and the Veneto www.arpav.veneto.it. Never set out on a long route if conditions are bad. Even a broad track can become treacherous in adverse weather, and high altitude terrain enveloped in

Beautifully located Rifugio Venezia (AV3)

thick mist makes orientation difficult. An altimeter is useful – when a known altitude (such as that of the refuge) goes up, this means the atmospheric pressure has dropped and the weather could change for the worse.

- Carry any rubbish back to the valley where it can be disposed of correctly; don't expect hut staff to deal with it. Organic waste such as apple cores and orange peel is best not left lying around as it upsets the diet of animals and birds.
- Be considerate when making a toilet stop. Keep away from watercourses, don't leave unsightly paper lying around and remember that abandoned huts and rock overhangs could serve as life-saving shelter for someone else!
- Collecting flowers, insects or minerals is strictly forbidden, as are fires.
- Carry extra protective clothing as well as energy foods for emergency situations. Remember that in normal circumstances the temperature drops an average of 6°C for every 1000m you climb.
- Learn the international call for help (page 37). **Do not rely on mobile phones**, as there may be no signal. In electrical storms, don't shelter under trees or rock overhangs and keep away from metallic fixtures.
- En route remember to collect the inked stamps from all rifugi you visit: present them to the Tourist Office at Belluno (AV1) and Feltre (AV2) for your badge and congratulations!
- Lastly, don't leave your common sense at home.

EMERGENCIES

For medical matters, walkers who live in the EU need a European Health Insurance Card (EHIC), which has replaced the old E111. Holders are entitled to free or subsidised emergency health treatment in Italy. UK residents can apply online at www.dh.gov.uk. Australia similarly has a reciprocal agreement – see www.medicareaustralia.gov.au.

Those from the US should make sure they have appropriate coverage.

Travel insurance to cover an alpine walking holiday is also strongly recommended as costs in the case of rescues can be hefty. Alpine club members (see Accommodation) are usually covered by a special policy.

Aiuto! (pronounced *eye-yoo-toh*) in Italian and *Zu Hilfe!* (pronounced *tsoo hilfer*) in German is Help!

The international rescue signals can come in handy: the call for help is **SIX** signals per minute. These can be visual (such as waving a handkerchief or flashing a torch) or audible (whistling or shouting). They are to be repeated after a one-minute pause. The answer is **THREE** visual or audible signals per minute, to be repeated after a one-minute pause. Anyone who sees or hears such a call for help must contact the nearest refuge, police station or the like as quickly as possible.

In Italy the general emergency telephone number is ☎ 112, while calls for *soccorso alpino* (mountain rescue) need to be made to ☎ 118.

The following arm signals could be useful for communicating with a helicopter:

- help needed
- land here
- YES (to pilot's question)

- help not needed
- do not land here
- NO (to pilot's question)

TREKKING IN THE DOLOMITES

A final **note on mobile phones:** it is tempting to be lulled into a false sense of security when carrying a mobile phone in the mountains. Be aware that relatively few high alpine places have signal. In contrast nearly all rifugi have a land-line telephone and experienced staff can always be relied on in emergencies.

USING THIS GUIDEBOOK

The routes have been divided into handy stages that correspond to a reasonable day's walking, concluding at a rifugio with meals and accommodation. However, these stages are only suggestions and the wonderful abundance of rifugi across the Dolomites means you can walk as much or as less as you like, varying the stage at will.

During the route description useful landmarks are given in **bold** with partial timing and altitude readings.

The heading for each stage contains the following essential information.

- **Time** – this does not include pauses for picnics, admiring views, photos and nature stops, so always add on a couple of hours to be realistic.
- **Distance** – in kilometres and miles. This is approximate and nowhere near as important as height gain or loss, which follow.
- **Ascent/Descent** – in metres (**NB** 100m=328ft).
- **Grade** gives an idea of the difficulty of the route. Remember that adverse weather conditions or snow cover will increase this.
  1 – a straightforward path with moderate gradient, suitable for all walkers
  2 – a fairly strenuous alpine walk, but not especially difficult
  3 – some experience on mountainous terrain is a prerequisite as there may be particularly steep and exposed sections, and a head for heights and orientation skills will come in useful.

ALTA VIA 1

Vast views above Portela del Piazedel (AV1 Stage 10)

TREKKING IN THE DOLOMITES

INTRODUCTION

Alta Via 1 (AV1) begins its memorable journey from the major artery Val Pusteria/Pustertal, which draws a line along the northernmost confine of the Dolomites. It is overshadowed by the imposing giants of western neighbours the Sesto group, which soar above dark green pine woods. Dobbiaco in the northwest has a handy youth hostel ☎ 0474 976216, http://dobbiaco.ostello.bz, and all the local villages have grocery shops.

Breaking off south halfway between Monguelfo and Villabassa is Valle di Braies, named for 'trousers' as the valley forks into 'legs', each with neat villages amidst manicured meadows. The southwestern branch concludes at a beautiful emerald green lake, Lago di Braies/Pragser Wildsee, and the official beginning of AV1. Popular for old-style boating it also boasts a marvellous alpine-style Grand Hotel built in 1899, and famous for hosting the Beatles' personal guru Maharishi Mahesh Yogi in the 1960s. Although it has seen better days, the Art Nouveau premises make a great place to stay and dine before setting out on the trek, and walkers are welcome. Hotel Lago di Braies ☎ 0474 748602, www.lagodibraies.com. Alongside is a café and souvenir shop in addition to a fee-paying car park (discount for long-term stays). With time to spare, it's worthwhile following the pretty ring route around the lake – allow 1hr 30min.

The lake's crystal-clear waters are bordered by shingle beaches, but the low temperatures discourage swimming – the surface rarely

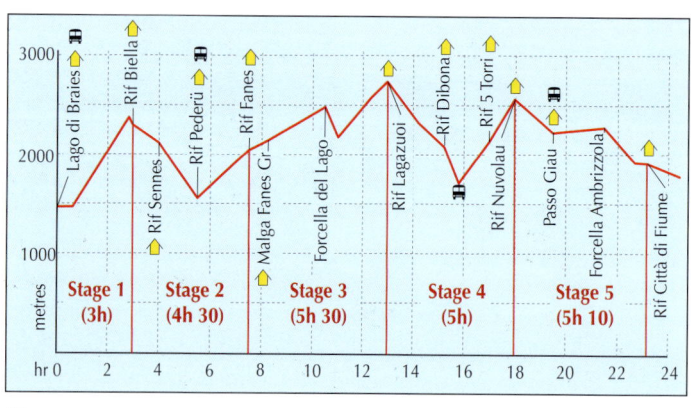

The terrace at Rifugio Coldai (Stage 6)

exceeds 14°C. In fact it usually ices over around November, reverting to liquid form in May but trout somehow survive in the chilly depths. Formed when the valley was obstructed by an ancient rock fall, Lago di Braies lies at the foot of sheer towering 2810m Croda del Becco/Seekofel reflected in the still waters. According to an old Ladin legend on a night with full moon once every hundred years, a curious sight may be witnessed: two women emerge through a secret doorway in the mountain the Ladins refer to as Sass dla Porta. Leaving their subjects to slumber in rocky caverns, Princess Dolasilla rows her blind mother the Queen of Fanes across the lake in the hope of silver trumpets announcing the dawning of the promised time for their doomed kingdom to be reborn. In vain for the time being it would seem.

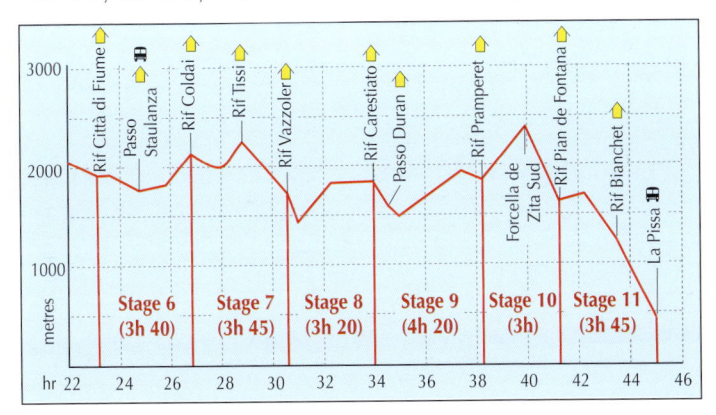

Trekking in the Dolomites

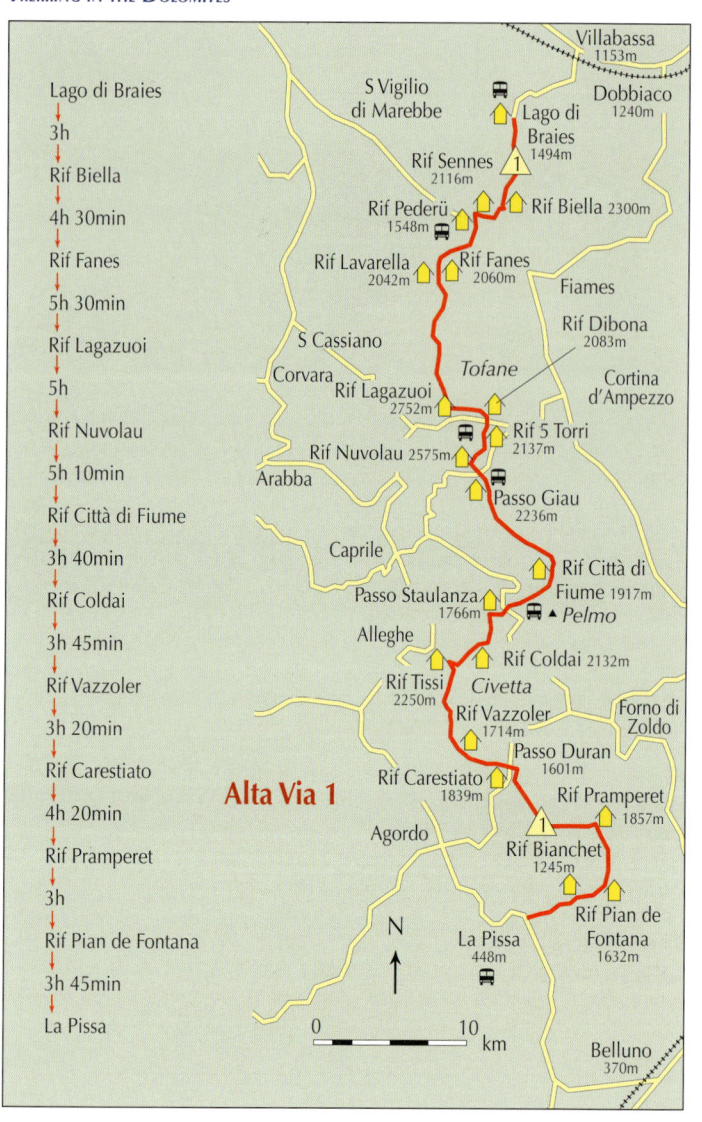

Lago di Braies
↓
3h
↓
Rif Biella
↓
4h 30min
↓
Rif Fanes
↓
5h 30min
↓
Rif Lagazuoi
↓
5h
↓
Rif Nuvolau
↓
5h 10min
↓
Rif Città di Fiume
↓
3h 40min
↓
Rif Coldai
↓
3h 45min
↓
Rif Vazzoler
↓
3h 20min
↓
Rif Carestiato
↓
4h 20min
↓
Rif Pramperet
↓
3h
↓
Rif Pian de Fontana
↓
3h 45min
↓
La Pissa

Alta Via 1

Villabassa 1153m
S Vigilio di Marebbe
Dobbiaco 1240m
Lago di Braies 1494m
Rif Sennes 2116m
Rif Pederü 1548m
Rif Biella 2300m
Rif Lavarella 2042m
Rif Fanes 2060m
Fiames
S Cassiano
Rif Dibona 2083m
Corvara
Tofane
Rif Lagazuoi 2752m
Cortina d'Ampezzo
Rif 5 Torri 2137m
Rif Nuvolau 2575m
Arabba
Passo Giau 2236m
Caprile
Rif Città di Fiume 1917m
Passo Staulanza 1766m
Pelmo
Alleghe
Rif Coldai 2132m
Rif Tissi 2250m
Civetta
Rif Vazzoler 1714m
Forno di Zoldo
Passo Duran 1601m
Rif Carestiato 1839m
Rif Pramperet 1857m
Agordo
Rif Bianchet 1245m
N
La Pissa 448m
Rif Pian de Fontana 1632m
0   10 km
Belluno 370m

STAGE 1
Lago di Braies to Rifugio Biella

Time	3hr
Distance	6.5km/4 miles
Ascent/Descent	870m/60m
Grade	2

Starting at a beautiful alpine lake set amidst pine forest and soaring Dolomite peaks, this is a thrilling opening to Alta Via 1. It entails a straightforward steady climb to a high altitude plateau that rewards walkers with wide-reaching vistas. In view of the relative brevity, walkers with energy to burn and a head for heights may like to fit in the ascent of 2810m Croda del Becco which flanks the hut – see below. On the other hand those desirous of a guesthouse – as opposed to the excellent but spartan rifugio at the official conclusion of Stage 1 – may care to proceed a further 1hr for Rifugio Sennes (see Stage 2).

The AV1 alias broad white gravel path n.1, makes a marvellous start from the **Hotel Lago di Braies** (1494m) in the realms of the Parco Naturale Fanes-Senes-Braies. On the lake's west bank it heads past a chapel along the water's edge, the massive bulk of the Croda del Becco ahead. This pretty stretch traverses squirrel-ridden woods close to the water's edge, the opposite shore dominated by the Grande and Piccolo Apostolo. Close to an attractive beach, ignore the fork R for **Val Foresta** and curve SE. Not far along the AV1 leaves this paradise, forking SSE (1496m, 35min) for the start of the 800m climb. The well-trodden path follows a scree river colonised by dwarf mountain pine, bilberry shrubs and mountain avens. The giant bulk of Croda del Becco towers overhead while marvellous views open up over Val Foresta W and its peaks. You wind steadily upwards, passing a 2034m **turn-off** for Malga Cavallo. Pretty shady wood precedes entry into a rock-strewn

TREKKING IN THE DOLOMITES

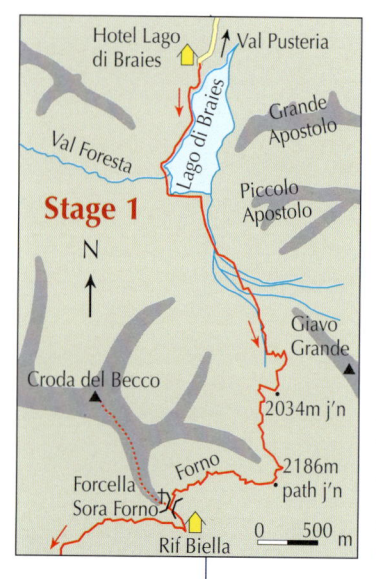

amphitheatre. Shortly, an imposingly steep barrier is surmounted on a straightforward zigzag route aided by fixed chains, only really necessary in wet or icy conditions. Here the sheer rock flanks bear clear signs of karstification, in the shape of grooves left by rainwater. In between are colourful patches of alpine blooms.

At a **path junction** (2186m, 1hr 35min) an abrupt fork R (W) marks the entry into the so-called **'Forno'** (oven) a heat trap as will quickly become evident to midsummer walkers. The clear path weaves its way between toppled rocks at the foot of Monte Muro on the final leg to

2hr 50min – Forcella Sora Forno (2388m) and a shrine. Entering the

Lago di Braies and the Grande Apostolo

STAGE 1 – LAGO DI BRAIES TO RIFUGIO BIELLA

Parco Naturale delle Dolomiti d'Ampezzo, the panorama is vast and breathtaking, from the most northerly Dolomite peak Sass de Putia W, close to the start of AV2, across to the Marmolada and its glittering glacier SW, taking in the Tofane pyramids, and the Pelmo S and Cristallo SE. For those who feel up to it and are not bothered by exposure, here begins the optional rewarding ascent of Croda del Becco.

Rifugio Biella and Croda del Becco

> **Side trip to Croda del Becco (2hr return)**
> From the pass a zigzagging path NW tackles an exposed corner with the help of cables set into the rock face. There are bird's-eye views onto Rifugio Biella. The flattish top will come as quite a surprise, as will the majestic if reticent ibex that graze here in summer. Over on the northern edge is the dizzy summit cross of **Croda del Becco** (2810m) directly over Lago di Braies. Simply breathtaking. Return the same way, taking special care on the exposed corner ridge.

A short way down the slope is

10min – Rifugio Biella aka Seekofel Hütte (2300m)
☎ 0436 866991, CAI, sleeps 45, open 3rd week in June to end Sept, www.rifugiobiella.it. This well-run hut has generous meals including a self-serve breakfast but only offers the bare essentials, which means a cold shower.

STAGE 2
Rifugio Biella to Rifugio Fanes

Time	4hr 30min
Distance	13.5km/8.4 miles
Ascent/Descent	630m/870m
Grade	1

AV1 crosses undulating rocky terrain on easy paths and 4WD tracks constructed for military purposes during WW1. Several privately run rifugi are touched on before a plunge to a road head, which entails losing an awful lot of height. Here is a rifugio, where refreshments are probably in order as you need to gird your loins – the day concludes with an extended uphill stretch terminating in a beautiful pasture basin with a choice of comfortable lodgings. **Note** The huts here are linked by rough roads and provide a jeep taxi service for needy guests.

From **Rifugio Biella** (2300m) set out W along the jeep route (n.6) below the remarkable onion layers that comprise the SE face of Croda del Becco. Just 10min on, AV1 departs ways with the track (which continues in a long leisurely loop stroll ESE around Col de Ra Sciores before veering due W for Rifugio Sennes – allow 1hr 15min). Branching uphill R (SW) path n.6 crosses knobbly grassy terrain punctuated with marmot burrows to reach the 2300m level. Re-entering the Parco Naturale Fanes-Senes-Braies, it drops to join another jeep track, thence L for

STAGE 2 – RIFUGIO BIELLA TO RIFUGIO FANES

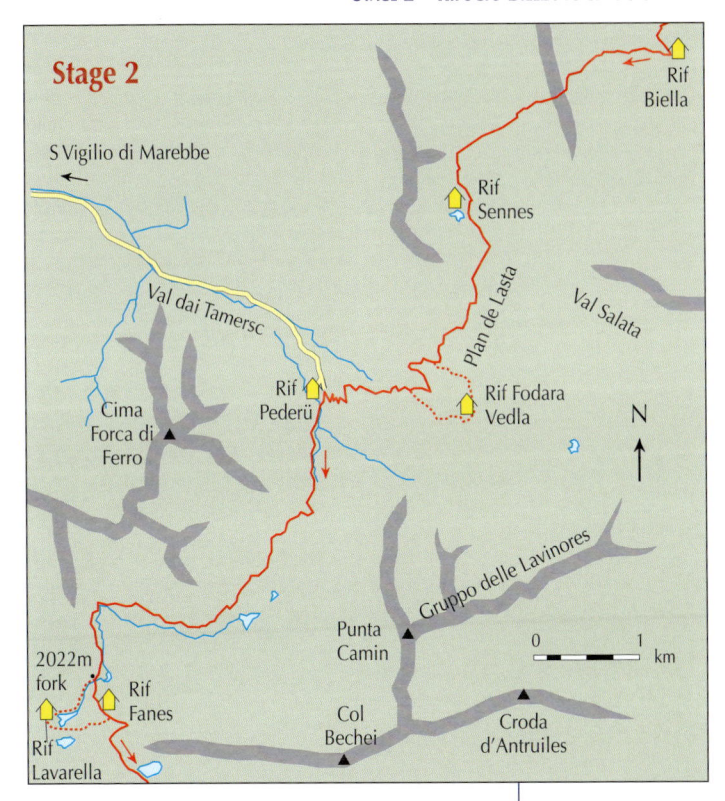

1hr – Rifugio Sennes aka Ücia de Senes (2116m)
☎ 0474 501092, private, sleeps 65, credit cards, open early June to mid-Oct, www.sennes.com. This place is popular with model plane enthusiasts and pilots thanks to the proximity of an airstrip, reputedly the highest in Europe for light craft!

Past the huddle of photogenic wood-tile roof shepherds' huts the track (n.7) proceeds S. Keep R at the ensuing fork and head SW over Plan de Lasta dotted with Arolla pines, and past a turn-off to **Rifugio Fodara Vedla**.

From here a short track leads W to rejoin the main AV1 route – an extra 15min should be allowed for this detour.

(The cosy family-run establishment occupies an enchanting position at 1966m; ☎ 0474 501093, private, sleeps 36, open mid-June to Oct, credit cards accepted, www.fodara.it). ◀

At ensuing forks, stick to the route signed for Pederü, soon a plunging descent W down steep mountainside. Later, in common with the access track for Rifugio Fodara Vedla, it becomes a knee-jarring white dirt road via a precipitous gully, the work of the military in the 1960s. Due W over the valley is jagged Cima Forca di Ferro, bright red for its iron content (*ferro*). Below in Val dai Tamersc is bustling café-guesthouse

1hr 30min – Rifugio Pederü (1548m). ☎ 0474 501086, sleeps 24, open June to Oct, credit cards, www.pederue.it. Summer SAD buses run to San Vigilio di Marebbe for connections to Val Pusteria (ⓘ 0474 501037, shops, hotels).

Rifugio Pederü in Val dai Tamersc

Next point your boots S. Walkers on the AV1 once risked being coated in thick dust from the jeep traffic,

STAGE 2 – RIFUGIO BIELLA TO RIFUGIO FANES

Rifugio Fanes

now thankfully a new path (n.7) branches R across the stream. It climbs the R side of the valley with its immense erosive spills colonised by dwarf mountain pine. The road is touched on briefly then you veer R over a rise. Due E are the scree flows tinged with red. Amidst the odd pine and low bushy vegetation the unsurfaced road is joined once and for all at the 1900m mark above the gushing stream Rio San Vigilio. An uphill stretch S emerges in a beautiful pasture basin dotted with old dark timber hay chalets and flanked by a curious series of limestone slab terracing dotted with conifers. This is known as the 'Marmot's Parliament' – a reference to the long-gone era of the legendary Kingdom of Fanes (see Stage 1 story). A 2022m fork L leads to

2hr – Rifugio Fanes (2060m). ☎ 0474 501097, private, sleeps 75, open mid-June to mid-Oct, www.rifugiofanes.com, credit cards taken. The atmosphere in this rambling establishment can verge on boisterous, making the nearby rifugio a quieter option.

Trekking in the Dolomites

> **Detour to Rifugio Lavarella**
> From the **2022m** fork in the road, continue straight on (SW) for 5min past a reedy lake to family-run **Rifugio Lavarella (2042m)**. ☎ 0474 501079, private, sleeps 45, open June to Oct, www.lavarella.it, credit cards accepted.
> At the rear of the building rises gently the sloping Sasso della Croce formation that culminates in Sasso delle Dieci and Sasso delle Nove. The next day take the path crossing the lake emissary and up NE through wood to join the track just above Rifugio Fanes – an extra 15min.

STAGE 3
Rifugio Fanes to Rifugio Lagazuoi

Time	5hr 30min
Distance	12km/7.5 miles
Ascent/Descent	1150m/450m
Grade	2

A laidback stroll along former military roads and across undulating stony pasture uplands becomes, little by little, more enthralling as all manner of Dolomites are approached. The Forcella del Lago marks AV1's entry into the dramatic and breathtaking Cortina Dolomites (not that it's been too bad thus far!). A steep gully is navigated on a much-improved path; an easier but longer variant via Rifugio Scotoni is given (walkers who opt for it may prefer to overnight there and continue with AV1 the following day). A tiring climb concludes at Rifugio Lagazuoi and, yes, is worth all the effort as this is an unrivalled vantage point when the weather is clear.

From **Rifugio Fanes (2060m)** path n.11 cuts the curves of the wide white gravel track and heads SE to open grassy **Passo di Limo (2175m, 10min)** with its old wood cross.

STAGE 3 – RIFUGIO FANES TO RIFUGIO LAGAZUOI

After Passo di Limo with Cime Campestrin

This spot affords great views E to Sasso della Croce as well as the smooth inclined slabs of Lavinores. Lago di Limo is passed, then AV1 breaks off R near abandoned military barracks in the vicinity of WW1 trenches. This slots into another track heading S with an inspiring outlook to spiral-form Cime Campestrin to the R of Vallon Bianco. Not far on is

45min – Malga Fanes Grande (2156m). This welcoming summer dairy farm does refreshments and simple meals, as well as dorm accommodation for 12 – sleeping bag essential; ☎ 346 2193374 or 349 3172061, open late June to 20 Sept, no shower.

Now with the massive Cunturines ahead SW, and even a peek of the snowbound Marmolada, AV1 proceeds SW on wide track n.11 across undulating pasture accompanied by a trickling stream, marmots and cows. Nearby on your R are the contorted folds and layers of Sass dei Bac and neighbours. Close to a turn-off for the Cunturines peak, **Passo Tadega (2143m)**

Trekking in the Dolomites

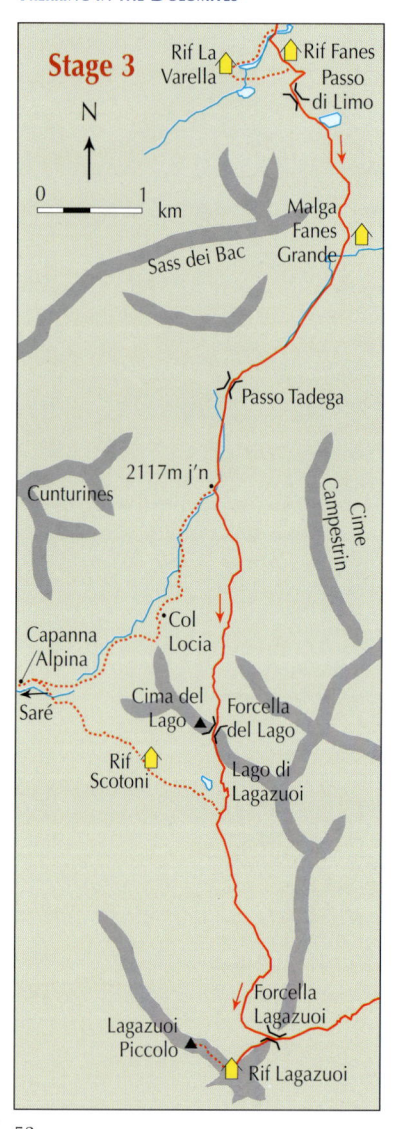

is encountered without event. A short distance S is a strategic if unnamed junction (2117m, 45min) where AV1 breaks off L on n.20B.

> **Variant via Rifugio Scotoni/ exit to Saré**
> A lovely, easier (if much longer) route, n.11 continues on the wide track to **Col Locia** (2069m) before descending SW via Plan de la Forca. You approach bar-restaurant **Capanna Alpina** (1hr 15min, 1726m, exit to the Valparola–San Cassiano road at 1652m **Saré** in a further 15min for hotels and SAD summer buses both directions). However, shortly before the place turn L (SE) for the main access path n.20 for the 1hr climb to **Rifugio Scotoni** (1985m) ☎ 0471 847330, private, sleeps 20, open late June to Sept, www.scotoni.it. Path n.20 continues uphill to Lago di Lagazuoi, and shortly afterwards joins the principal AV1 route (30min).

It's a steady climb with stunning views to the Sella and Marmolada, the route of AV2. The clear path is heading for a notch between Cima del Lago and Punte di Fanes, namely

STAGE 3 – RIFUGIO FANES TO RIFUGIO LAGAZUOI

2hr 15min – Forcella del Lago (2486m). Straight ahead is the smooth profile of Lagazuoi Piccolo. However, at your feet a plunging, stomach-dropping gully is revealed. But fear not, as the recently restored path is good if narrow. It zigzags madly downhill, aided by sturdy timber reinforcements. Below lies glittering green Lago di Lagazuoi. You exit the gully keeping L (S), high above the lake. Ignore the turn-offs R and traverse scree to the bleached stone ruins of a wartime building. Here, at approx. 2220m (30min), you turn L onto broad path n.20 and the variant from Rifugio Scotoni. This immense grey rock incline is known as the Alpe di Lagazuoi, but only the odd chamois grazes here. It is bordered ahead SE by the wall of Lagazuoi Grande whereas due S is Lagazuoi Piccolo, the entire area the arena of fighting and terrible loss of life during the 1914–18 conflict. Bearing witness still today on these slopes are the scattered timbers, remains of trench systems and even cabins for the aerial goods cableway supply systems. These will serve as distractions from the ascent that awaits: clearly visible 500m above is the cable-car arrival station close to today's destination – and it never feels any closer over the ensuing hour or so!

The Parco Naturale Fanes-Senes-Braies is left behind, as you enter the Parco Naturale delle Dolomiti d'Ampezzo. Further up the earlier military nature of the track becomes clear, with stone edging. Moreover, a ghost village is passed, its WW1 huts all but crumbled to the ground. Soon you emerge at

1hr 50min – Forcella Lagazuoi (2573m). Views to the Averau, Nuvolau and Pelmo, future stages of AV1.

Turn R for the final slog, tight zigzags up the L side of a bulldozed winter ski piste, past caverns and positions dating back to WW1. A tad above the **cable-car station** is the highest point on AV1, namely

40min – Rifugio Lagazuoi (2752m). ☎ 0436 867303, private, sleeps 74, open 20 June to 10 Oct, credit cards,

TREKKING IN THE DOLOMITES

Stunning position of Rifugio Lagazuoi

www.rifugiolagazuoi.com. Clouds permitting, the renowned panoramic terrace will provide breathtaking views to enjoy with that well-earned beer.

Extension to Piccolo Lagazuoi (30min return)
From the terrace, a clear path proceeds WNW along a narrow ridge, with a guiding handrail at first. The crest broadens, culminating at a huge cross marking the actual peak of **Piccolo Lagazuoi** (2778m).

Note The cable-car runs down to Passo Falzarego (2105m) where a bus (Dolomiti Bus) can be caught to the posh resort of Cortina d'Ampezzo ⓘ 0436 3231/2/3; good range of shops and hotels, as well as onward bus transport.

STAGE 4
Rifugio Lagazuoi to Rifugio Nuvolau

Time	5hr
Distance	14km/8.7 miles
Ascent/Descent	900m/1080m
Grade	2

Whichever way you go, this stage is of great interest for both the spectacular mountains around and the abundance of reminders of the terrible years of World War One, due to the vicinity of the former border between the long-dismantled Hapsburg Empire and Italy. The main AV1 route embarks on a memorable traverse below the awesome Tofana di Rozes. After a hospitable rifugio, it drops to the Cortina–Passo Falzarego road then climbs through forest to the fascinating, renowned Cinque Torri area, with a magnificent conclusion at lookout par excellence Rifugio Nuvolau.

However, there are difficult decisions to be made! For anyone with a sense of adventure and no problems with vertigo or claustrophobia, a strongly recommended variant explores the Lagazuoi wartime rock tunnels and cuts dramatically down to Passo Falzarego. Afterwards is a fair climb skirting the Averau to a cosy rifugio where the main route is joined for the final leg to Nuvolau.

A final note The start of Stage 5 entails several clambers and a short aided stretch down an exposed path to Passo Giau. This can be detoured by choosing the easy variant from Rifugio Scoiattoli, bypassing Nuvolau.

During the 1914–18 conflict Piccolo Lagazuoi was occupied by the troops of the Austro-Hungarian Empire – it is important to remember that at that time Cortina d'Ampezzo was one of the southernmost parts of the Empire, so this was the front as the Italians advanced. Both sides spent massive amounts of time, energy and human lives excavating daring tunnels (11 in all) through the mountains for the purpose of laying explosives to mine ▶

enemy positions. The scars can still be seen. Tunnels have been restored for visitors with helpful info boards en route illustrating living conditions and supply route, including the 1100m-long, 45°, 230m height difference Galleria Lagazuoi described below.

Excavated by the Italians from their stronghold on the Cengia Martini, it was designed to dislodge the Austrians who occupied the summit. Nowadays the entire area is an open-air museum illustrated with graphic reminders of the ordeal both sides endured. More lives were lost through avalanches than actual fighting.

From **Rifugio Lagazuoi** (2752m) walk down the steps to the **cable-car station**. Here starts the variant route via the wartime tunnels – sure-footed walkers equipped with a headlamp: be warned, it can be slippery. Gloves can be handy as the cable handrail is cold. **A final note** For a modest fee you may prefer to send your rucksack down to the pass by cable-car.

Exploring the Lagazuoi tunnels

STAGE 4 – RIFUGIO LAGAZUOI TO RIFUGIO NUVOLAU

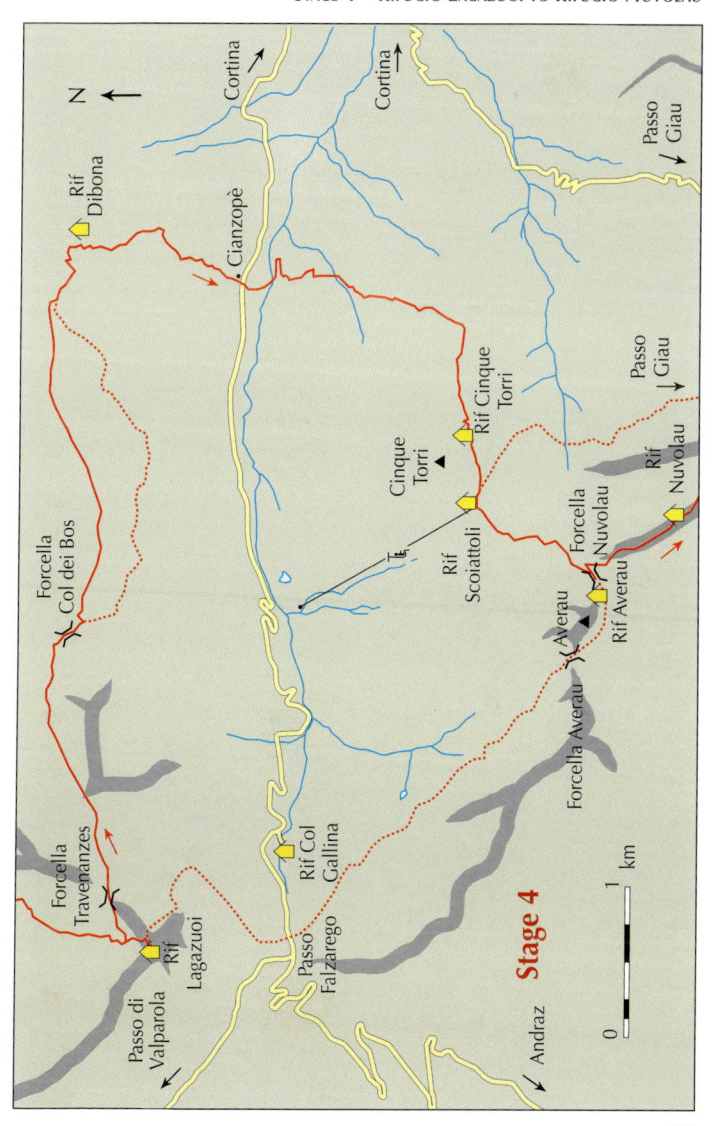

Variant via wartime tunnels, Passo Falzarego to Rifugio Averau (3hr)

Follow the arrows for 'G' (*galleria* is Italian for 'tunnel') leading below the concrete platform and L (E) via trenches and a narrow crest. The actual tunnel entrance (10min) is a timber doorway where the path 'disappears' into a hole. A glance down into the semi-darkness gives a good idea of what's to come! A cable handrail is reassuring as it's often slippery underfoot due to the constant presence of water on the steps and ladders. A string of rock 'windows' provide dizzying views and occasional natural light. En route are reconstructed storage depots, cramped sleeping quarters and eerie passageways.

After 1hr of knee-jarring descent, you exit onto a broad ledge adjoining **Cengia Martini**, a former Italian stronghold. Proceed L via a snow-choked gully and final short tunnel then a zigzag path to join path n.402 and the final drop to **Passo Falzarego** (2105m, 1hr 30min). The name for this well-visited road pass comes from 'false king': the erstwhile head of the intriguing legendary kingdom of Fanes traded his realm for prized treasures. His pact with the enemy turned sour and the traitor turned into rock – his stone-frozen profile with flowing beard and a crown of rocky points clearly recognisable.

Cafés, restaurants, tantalising souvenirs, buses to Val Badia (SAD), Cortina, Alleghe and Belluno (Dolomiti Bus). The closest accommodation is 10min down the road E: privately owned guesthouse **Rifugio Col Gallina** (2054m) ☎ 0436 2939, sleeps 25, open mid-June to late Sept, rifugio.colgallina@dolomiti.org.

On the S side of the pass path n.441 strikes out SE across red clay slopes and flowered meadows, which give way to calcareous terrain brightened by yellow poppies. A series of shallow gullies follows as the going becomes steeper. A variant from Rifugio Col Gallina merges close to **Forcella Averau** (2435m, 1hr 10min), haunt of amazing numbers of jet-black alpine choughs. Vast panoramas accompany the scree path SE skirting the crumbling southern wall of Averau to **Forcella Nuvolau** with **Rifugio Averau** (2413m, 20min), and the main AV1 route.

Continue down to **Forcella Lagazuoi** (2573m, 30min) as per the ascent route. Turn R onto n.402-1 beneath a stark red mountainside and heavy-duty avalanche barriers. Ahead NE rise the massive Tofane, while clustered to the E is the vast spread of the Cortina Dolomites. Quickly

STAGE 4 – RIFUGIO LAGAZUOI TO RIFUGIO NUVOLAU

reached is **Forcella Travenanzes** (2507m), and an exit path for Passo Falzarego. AV1 proceeds across the head of the immense trough of Val Travenanzes, ignoring turn-offs. Grassy-stony terrain is traversed in slight descent to

1hr 15min – Forcella Col dei Bos (2331m) with its WW1 memorial 'decorated' with period barbed wire and rusty tins. Towering overhead is the ill-famed Castelletto spur, hotly contested during the war and devastated by explosives in the summer of 1916, resulting in huge loss of life.

Due S are the recognisable shapes of the shattered blocks of the Cinque Torri, with Averau and Nuvolau. Fork R on n.402 in gradual descent along the lines of trenches. Confusingly, two more signs announce Forcella Col dei Bos at slightly lower altitudes. At the third (2290m), turn L (E) onto n.404.

The Cinque Torri backed by the Pomagagnon

TREKKING IN THE DOLOMITES

> **Lower path variant**
> This alternative route crosses to **Rifugio Dibona** at a lower altitude, but the timing is the same. Ignoring the forks L for Castelletto, keep R downhill with brilliant views to the Cinque Torri backed by the vast flat slabs of Laston di Formin and jagged, teethy Croda da Lago. At an old military road (Rozes junction 2183m), turn L on n.412 for a pretty, if narrow, traverse E through woodland. (**Note** If you don't need the hut facilities, by all means take the path 15min prior to Rifugio Dibona – it's signed for '5 Torri' – it turns S for the road, where the main route can be picked up.) Continue onto a jeep track for amazing views up into the eroded gully to the **Valon de Tofana** junction (2120m, 50min), continuing in common with the main (upper) route.

Climbing a little, it skirts the awesome southern base of the Tofana di Rozes, passing a branch (2400m) for the Galleria del Castelletto (by all means climb up to view the entrance to the war tunnel, now restored and the start of a via ferrata route). Further along this incredibly scenic path, n.442 forks R downhill across an immense eroded gully between the Tofane, where rock needles seemingly grow out of sand! Past a cableway load point is the **Valon de Tofana** junction (2120m). Continue 10min on the jeep track down to

Named after Angelo Dibona, a famous turn-of-the-century guide and mountaineer from Cortina, the hut serves as a strategic base for climbers on the Tofane.

1hr – Rifugio Dibona (2083m) ☎ 0436 860294, private, sleeps 70, open 15 June to 20 Sept, credit cards. ◄

Down the gravel road, n.442 forks R at the first bend. The steep path traverses beautiful conifer wood with roe deer and clearings of meadow saffron. The road from Cortina is crossed at

35min – Cianzopè (1724m) with bus stops (Dolomiti Bus) for both directions. (To save 300m in ascent, by all means go 2km up the road for the effort-free chair lift ride to Rifugio Scoiattoli.)

Straight across is n.439, initially surfaced. A path soon breaks off climbing steadily S through wood and eventually emerges on the edge of an ancient landslide,

STAGE 4 – RIFUGIO LAGAZUOI TO RIFUGIO NUVOLAU

a superb viewing point over the Cortina basin. Soon a broader track is joined – turn R (W) for cosy old-style

Lovely position of Rifugio Cinque Torri

1hr 10min – Rifugio Cinque Torri (2137m). ☎ 0436 2902, privately owned, sleeps 24, open 10 June to 30 Sept, www.cinquetorri.it.

It's worth detouring here to explore the maze of positions, fortifications, trenches and smaller rock formations that snake below the crazy Cinque Torri (five towers). In 2004 one of the surrounding minor towers dramatically collapsed. Acrobatic rock climbers provide spectacular performances on the five main towers.

The path climbs a little further to the arrival of the chair lift at splendidly placed cheery **Rifugio Scoiattoli** (2225m, 10min) ☎ 0436 867939, privately run, sleeps 25, open July to Sept, rifugio.scoiattoli@dolomiti.org. The name 'squirrels' is for the famous Cortina team of rock climbers.

Note Walkers who prefer to avoid the aided sections at the start of Stage 5 should turn off here, bypassing Rifugio Nuvolau. It's a delightful route and little-visited.

Trekking in the Dolomites

> **Direct route to Passo Giau (1hr 20min)**
> Clear path n.443 cuts SE across grassy slopes on a roller coaster course skirting the eastern flank of Nuvolau. Veritable meadows of rich globe flowers give way to rockier terrain, home to marmots and chamois. Curious vestiges of an ancient wall are encountered: the Muraglia di Giau was erected in the 1700s to mark the divide between neighbouring Cadore and Ampezzo communities locked in drawn-out bitter feuds over grazing rights. With inspiring views onto flat-topped Laston di Formin, the path bears S, slotting into the main AV1 and dropping finally to **Passo Giau** (2236m – see Stage 5).

A straightforward track leads to a saddle and **Rifugio Averau** (2413m) ☎ 0436 4660, privately run, sleeps 21, open beg. June to end Sept, accepts credit cards, rifugio.averau@dolomiti.org. Some of the best cuisine on AV1 is served on a terrace with brilliant views to the Marmolada and its shrinking glacier. Don't miss the *casunziei*, delicately flavoured ravioli stuffed with beetroot and served with melted butter and poppy seeds.

Adjacent is an unusual broad incline alias path n.439 up the Nuvolau to the amazing perch of

1hr – Rifugio Nuvolau (2575m) ☎ 0436 867938, CAI, sleeps 25, open 15 June to 30 Sept, siorpaes@yahoo.com. While creature comforts are scarce here (the bathroom's outside and has no shower or warm water), the extraordinary position and hospitality make up for it. Waking up for the dawn colours is a must, especially if the mount is not living up to its name – *nuvola* means 'cloud'. A hut was first built here in the early 1800s thanks to a donation left by a wealthy baron from Dresden, in recognition for help in recovering from a serious illness. Due to artillery damage during WW1, it had to be rebuilt by the local Alpine Club. A bridle track opened the way for fashionable ladies on horseback. And the views? Not enough space here to list them all.

STAGE 5
Rifugio Nuvolau to Rifugio Città di Fiume

Time	5hr 10min
Distance	12km/7.5 miles
Ascent/Descent	400m/1050m
Grade	2–3

Quite an amazing series of Dolomite landscapes are encountered today in a superb succession of peaks and ranges. The stage begins with a short via ferrata of aided passages to get you over the rocky realms of the Nuvolau – average difficulty in good conditions. Having crossed the road pass Passo Giau, a few more moderate climbs lead to a magnificent open pasture basin, once the hunting ground of Mesolithic men. Panoramas are non-stop as a brilliant line-up of Dolomites comes into view – as the Tofane are left behind, the Pelmo is the undisputed king of the day, but the Civetta comes a close second at day's end. Walkers in need of mod cons and a bit of luxury should plan on overshooting Rifugio Città di Fiume by an extra 1hr 30min, to overnight at Passo Staulanza – see Stage 6.

From **Rifugio Nuvolau** (2575m), just past the flagpole, path n.438 disappears over the edge of the short ridge, dropping with the aid of firmly anchored cable to easier terrain. With an eye out for the red/white waymarking, head SE across undulating rock surface, ignoring a higher variant to the Ra Gusela summit. A pole at the far edge of the plateau marks the start of a second aided section, beginning with a brief ledge and descending a crumbly, moderately exposed gully with more cable. At the bottom marshy meadows are soon gained (the direct route from Rifugio Scoiattoli links in here) for the saunter down the slope to join the bikers at

1hr 30min – Rifugio Passo Giau (2236m). Meals, coffee shop and hotel with mod cons, privately owned, rather

Across the top of Nuvolau

Bid farewell to the Tofane and enjoy the beautiful pasture amphitheatre on hand, backed by the rearing Pelmo, impressive and much closer now.

unreliable, ☎ 0437 720130, sleeps 17, open June to Sept, www.passogiau.it. Summer Dolomiti Bus to Cortina.

Cross the road for path n.436, pass a chapel and begin uphill to the rear of grassy knoll Col Piombin, the name from 'lead' is a sign of long-gone mining activity. With plenty of ups and downs, the narrow way leads across the head of Val Cernera towards a notable fault line with gashes of dramatically contrasting coloured rocks as you clamber up to **Forcella Giau** (2360m, 1hr). ◀ Under the sheer face of the Laston di Formin, the AV1 traverses Mondeval di Sora, bordered on the eastern edge by isolated Becco di Mezzodì.

Chattering choughs and felt-leaved edelweiss abound. Mesolithic hunters were known to have closed off the five passes entering the basin so as to trap wild animals such as elk, ibex and deer in combined tribal summer hunts. An encampment was located at a landmark over-sized boulder further on. The path drops to cross streams, then gains the earthy saddle

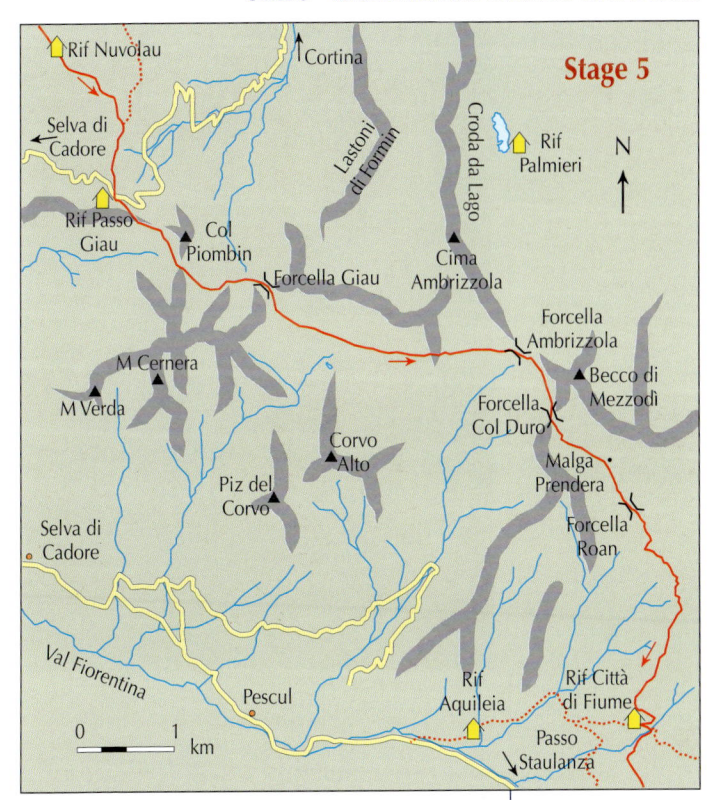

Stage 5 – Rifugio Nuvolau to Rifugio Città di Fiume

2hr – Forcella Ambrizzola (2277m). Here the vast outlook spaces over the Cortina basin to the Pomagagnon (NW) and adjoining Cristallo.

Still on n.436 you coast S amidst a chaos of fallen rocks and boulders below Becco di Mezzodì to a minor pass **Forcella Col Duro** and the gentle descent to the abandoned stalls of **Malga Prendera** (2148m). With views to the majestic Sorapiss, unmistakable pyramid of Antelao and far-off Cadore Dolomites, in a SSE direction on n.458 continue downhill to **Forcella Roan** (2075m),

65

The Pelmo looms above Rifugio Città di Fiume

usually a favourite hang-out of cows. A final uphill stretch on n.467 goes through light wood, then all of a sudden the Pelmo is incredibly close, at this range it's easy to understand why it was dubbed 'Throne of the Gods'. At your feet in pretty Val Fiorentina is

1hr 40min – Rifugio Città di Fiume (1917m) ☎ 0437 720268, CAI, sleeps 25, open 15 June to 20 Sept, www.rifugiocittadifiume.it. Water not suitable for drinking. ◄ This massive mountain, isolated on all flanks and recognisable from afar for its armchair shape, rises dizzily to 3168m from scree slopes. The first recorded ascent, in 1857, was by British pioneer mountaineer and founder of the Alpine Club, John Ball, but prehistoric hunters probably got there a bit earlier.

Don't miss the spicy goulash stew – or the golden sunset on the Pelmo for that matter.

STAGE 6 – RIFUGIO CITTÀ DI FIUME TO RIFUGIO COLDAI

Curiously, the hut is the property of the Italian Alpine Club branch once located in Fiume, now known as Rijeka, a port town in Croatia. The border shifted post-WW2, but the name lives on.

> **Exit route** A farm lane drops to the road in Val Fiorentina in about 45min. Another heads W via Rifugio Aquileia and camping ground. Both are handy for the summer bus on the Longarone–Passo Staulanza–Caprile runs (Dolomiti Bus).

STAGE 6
Rifugio Città di Fiume to Rifugio Coldai

Time	3hr 40min
Distance	9.3km/5.8 miles
Ascent/Descent	520m/300m
Grade	2

After a spectacular traverse that gives walkers ample time to appreciate the Pelmo from close quarters, the main AV1 route makes its straightforward way via a road pass and up for a stiff climb to a superbly run alpine hut, Rifugio Coldai, in the realms of another awesome stone giant, the Civetta – more about that when the time comes. However, a highly recommended variant Sentiero Flaibani embarks on a steep rather difficult climb, part of a rewarding loop around the stone giant Pelmo itself, taking in beautifully placed Rifugio Venezia. Requirements are the confidence to cover uncertain terrain and not being bothered by heights. Perfect weather is key as the gullies encountered are subject to rockfalls. Some snow is likely in early summer. Longer than the main route, it can be interrupted at Palafavera. The two routes meet up at Casera Pioda.

A final note Groceries are sold at the Palafavera camping ground encountered on the variant.

TREKKING IN THE DOLOMITES

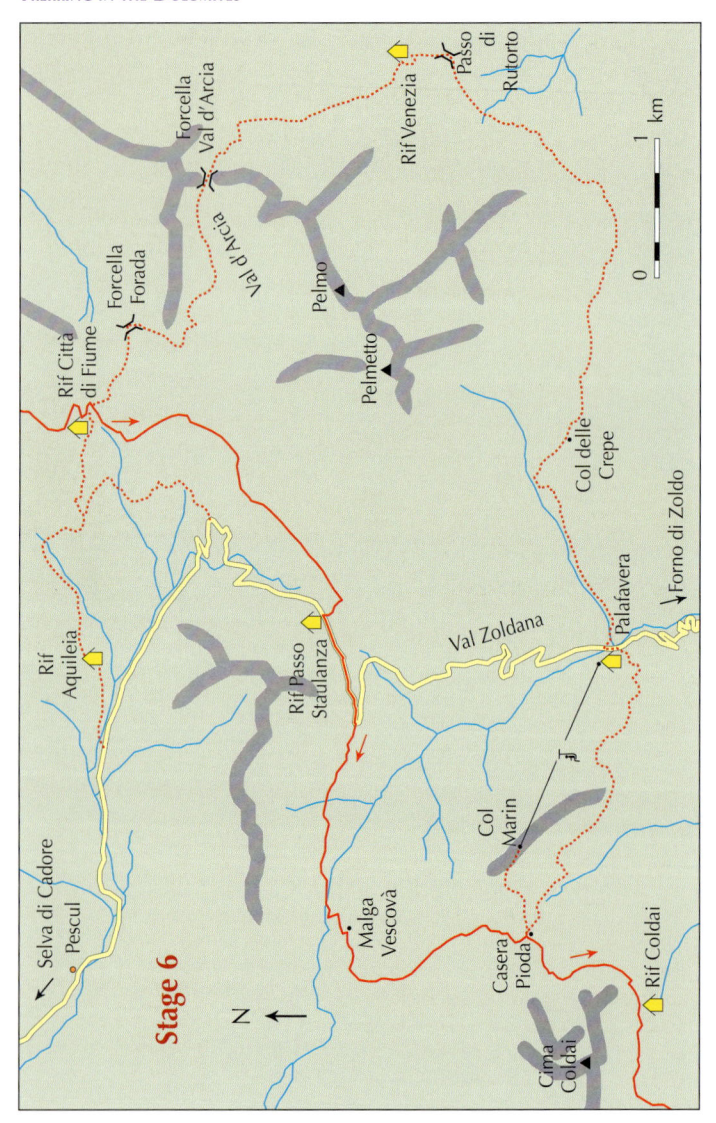

STAGE 6 – RIFUGIO CITTÀ DI FIUME TO RIFUGIO COLDAI

From **Rifugio Città di Fiume** (1917m), at the first bend of the jeep track turn off across a bridge then turn sharp R on path n.472 in descent through light larch wood heading mostly S. (Don't be tempted by the path straight ahead uphill – it's the start of the variant – see below.) You soon find yourself on the lower fringe of a yawning scree spread at the base of Val d'Arcia, dwarfed by the Pelmo, where snow lingers below the 3168m peak. Curving SW you cross a zone of low mountain pine before surmounting a minor crest. Keep R at the forks, and it's not far down to the creature comforts of

1hr 30min – Rifugio Passo Staulanza (1766m). ☎ 0437 788566, private establishment run by a mountaineer, sleeps 50, open 10 June to 30 Sept, www.staulanza.it. It means a pricey stay but the meals are delicious and it serves the best breakfast on the AV1! Summer Dolomiti Bus runs to Forno di Zoldo in Val Zoldana (ⓘ 0437 787349 and hotels such as Hotel Mae ☎ 0437 789189, www.hotelmae.com).

Signposts on the way to Malga Vescovà

Head down the road. At the first bend (1715m) turn R (W) onto the lane into forest. Further along it's L at the colourful cluster of signposts. Amidst beautiful pasture stands **Malga Vescovà** (1734m, 30min), a farm that does meals and refreshments. Here AV1 forks L off the lane for path n.561, climbing the hillside SW. A long level saddle (1876m) precedes a dirt road under Roa Bianca and avalanche barriers. A path soon cuts down to summer farm

1hr 10min – Casera Pioda aka Malga Pioda (1812m). Drinking fountain, dairy products and refreshments occasionally on sale. The Pelmo variant slots in at this point.

Pelmo variant (6hr)

Leave **Rifugio Città di Fiume** (1917m) on n.480 which branches L from the signposted junction on the lane below the building. After crossing the stream a wide path ascends gently through wood to **Forcella Forada** (1977m). Here, turn sharp R (S) on a narrow unmarked path which descends a little. It is not always clear and may be obstructed by springy mountain pines. A chaotic erosion channel is traversed. Soon the strategic steep-sided gully is reached (n.480 on rock) where the Sentiero Flaibani forks L (E) for a tiring clamber that feels near vertical at times. Guided by red paint splashes and occasionally observed by chamois, after a fair slog the path goes L for a section aided by cable and rungs over polished slippery rock. It emerges on a breathtaking crest with a bird's-eye view of the rifugio and much more. A much improved path leads NE below Cima Forada. A grassy ridge frequented by marmots is gained on the N edge of awesome **Val d'Arcia**. Keep L (NW) through an overwhelming jungle of tumbled rocks and scree, where mere walkers are dwarfed. Red paint splashes need to be followed carefully. Surprisingly bright clumps of Rhaetian poppies flourish in this wilderness. After hugging the rock face at the base of Cima Val d'Arcia you cross towards the R side of this immense valley and ascend very steeply, finally gaining

2hr 15min – Forcella Val d'Arcia (2476m). As you get your breath back it's hard to know which way to look first! Back W is the Marmolada, NW the terraced Sella massif, while ahead E is the unmistakable triangle of Antelao, and beyond SE spiky Spalti di Toro. This dizzy perch is the haunt of perpetually hungry alpine choughs, which beg for scraps.

STAGE 6 – RIFUGIO CITTÀ DI FIUME TO RIFUGIO COLDAI

Now brace your knees for the descent. The path disappears dramatically over the edge but take heart as the rubble base is soft and, once you dig your heels in, descending is quite straightforward. Heading ESE it rounds a rock face guided by fixed cables, handy for the narrow passages on crumbly terrain. After a minor saddle the path improves and with the rifugio in sight is accompanied by a multitude of wildflowers. Skirting beneath the Pelmo's prominent Spalla Est (east shoulder) you drop to

1hr – Rifugio Venezia (1947m). ☎ 0436 9684, CAI, sleeps 60, open 20 June to 20 Sept. Memorable sunsets, home-made tarts and hearty soups. The hut dates back to 1892, and is currently run by an alpine guide who accompanies visitors on the *via normale* to the Pelmo summit.

After nearby **Passo di Rutorto** (1931m), AV1 heads decidedly SW as path n.472 drops across a rocky basin beneath towering walls. A climb through light wood to a marshy saddle sees the route bear W, mostly on a level and immersed in dwarf mountain pines. At **Col delle Crepe** (1885m) fork L (mostly SW) following Rio Bianco and path n.474 through forest to the road at

1hr 45min – Palafavera (1507m). Groceries at the camping ground, and two privately run rifugi: Rifugio Palafavera ☎ 0437 789133-789472, sleeps 25, open mid-June to mid-Sept, www.palafavera.com; Rifugio Monte Pelmo ☎ 0437 789359, sleeps 9, open mid-June to early Sept. Summer buses (Dolomiti Bus) run down to Forno di Zoldo ⓘ 0437 787349.

A chair lift can be used on the next section in lieu of the rather uninteresting motorable farm road W up through forest, although several short cuts can be taken. (The lift terminates at 1889m Col Marin, thereafter is a 10min link path).

1hr – Casera Pioda aka Malga Pioda (1816m) and the main AV1 route.

Popular path n.556 starts uphill, the zigzags of the wartime mule track taking the sting from the steepness. The east shoulder of Cima Coldai is gradually rounded as the Civetta is approached. Shortly after a goods cableway is

1hr – Rifugio Coldai (2132m). ☎ 0437 789160, CAI, sleeps 83, open mid-June to 20 Sept, barance@dolomiti.com. A superb hut run by a hospitable local family for

The Pelmo over Passo Staulanza

the last 40 years. They whip up delicious apple strudel and wholesome meals for starving walkers. Wonderful vantage point for sunsets on the Pelmo, so make sure you score a seat near the window.

STAGE 7
Rifugio Coldai to Rifugio Vazzoler

Time	3hr 45min
Distance	9.5km/6 miles
Ascent/Descent	380m/800m
Grade	2

An easy-going and absolutely brilliant stage spent appreciating the phenomenal Civetta, one of the most impressive Dolomite formations. Shaped like an enormous trident and likened to a set of organ pipes, it rises majestically between the deep-cut Cordevole river valley and smiling pasture of Val Zoldana. The slender rock barrier extends N–S for 6km, the southern extremity linked to the Moiazza, as will be seen in Stage 8. Soaring to 3220m, it was first scaled by British mountaineer Francis Fox Tuckett in 1867. En route today, halfway along the western wall is a lookout par excellence, Rifugio Tissi; it's well worth considering an overnight stay here for one of the most spectacular sunsets in the whole of the Dolomites.

STAGE 7 – RIFUGIO COLDAI TO RIFUGIO VAZZOLER

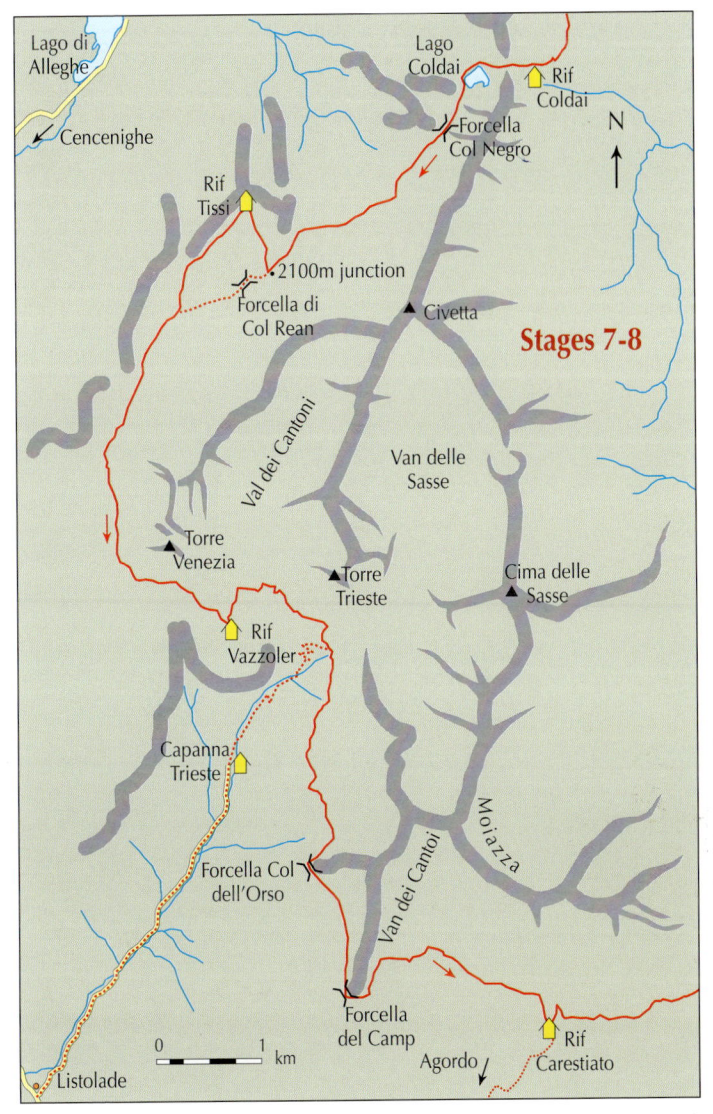

From **Rifugio Coldai** (2132m), n.560 leads W over a rise to a vision of the Marmolada and Sella, along with pretty green **Lago Coldai**. A popular picnic spot, it also boasts diminutive beaches and the temptation to take the plunge is strong. Amidst a veritable web of paths, AV1 skirts the R shore of the lake, ignores a turn-off for Alleghe and climbs S via the notch of **Forcella Col Negro** (2203m) for your first close-up of the majestic west 'wall of walls' and Val Civetta. Ricocheting rock discharges resound of an afternoon, so stick to the safe main routes and **don't be tempted by higher short cuts** – most disappear in any case, obliterated by debris, obliging walkers to awkward clambering. Despite the chaotic scree, mountain avens and yellow poppies flourish here.

AV1 loses a fair bit of height on this tiring descent with loose stones. The good news is that there are bird's-eye views to Alleghe and its green lake, formed in the 1700s after a mammoth landslip descended from the polished oblique slab clearly visible. An uphill leg reaches a well-marked **2100m junction** for Rifugio Tissi. Only if time is tight (a saving of 30min) should this be missed to continue to nearby **Forcella di Col Rean** (2107m) and onwards.

Alleghe and its lake come into sight a long way below

Stage 7 – Rifugio Coldai to Rifugio Vazzoler

2hr – Rifugio Tissi (2250m). ☎ 0437 721644, CAI, sleeps 65, open 25 June to 25 Sept, rifugio.tissi@gmail.it. While the water is not suitable for drinking, the beer certainly is!

Rifugio Vazzoler

Towards evening the hut empties as the sun goes down, as everyone heads up the hill (Cima di Col Rean) to the cross to drink in the divine technicolour show.

Resume the AV1 without returning to the 2100m junction but heading S to Val Civetta and n.560. Soon there's soft grassy terrain, a comfort for the feet after all that scree, but watch out for mud. The vegetation picks up too with larch, juniper and pink spreads of alpenrose, across a pasture plain with derelict Cason di Col Rean. Gigantic stone cubes lie in the shadow of soaring Torre Venezia, the point of the eastern trident. As the path rounds this southernmost corner of the Civetta, the fairytale turrets and spires of the Moiazza appear SE through the trees, topped by Moiazza Nord. A gravelly farm road is soon reached (turn L) for the final 15min to the beautiful conifer wood where is ensconced

Trekking in the Dolomites

1hr 45min – Rifugio Vazzoler (1714m) ☎ 0437 660008, CAI, sleeps 80, open 20 June to 20 Sept, vazzoler@email. it. Lovely alpine botanical garden that boasts both common and rare specimens. Inside the hut a model of the Civetta aids in understanding the layout of the giant. This relaxed rambling rifugio stands at the base of Val dei Cantoni with the twin rock bastions Torre Venezia and Torre Trieste guarding their respective corners.

Exit route to Listolade (2hr)
The jeep track (n.555) that serves the hut can be followed in descent S to Val Corpassa and homely **Capanna Trieste** (☎ 0437 660122, sleeps 25, open May to November, www.rifugiocapannatrieste.com) that does divine gnocchi with smoked ricotta. Narrow but surfaced from here on, the lane continues to the main road at **Listolade** (701m) for a bar/restaurant and year-round buses (Dolomiti Bus) to Belluno or Alleghe.

STAGE 8
Rifugio Vazzoler to Rifugio Carestiato

Time	3hr 20min
Distance	9km/5.6 miles
Ascent/Descent	600m/480m
Grade	2+

This stage progresses at lower altitudes on the edge of forest and scree beneath a breathtaking line-up of soaring rock walls and towers belonging to the Siamese twinned Civetta and Moiazza groups. Height gain and loss are relatively small; the stage can feasibly be extended to Passo Duran (Stage 9) for more accommodation options.

Leave **Rifugio Vazzoler** (1714m) on the white gravel track that curves NE at first through conifer cover

STAGE 8 – RIFUGIO VAZZOLER TO RIFUGIO CARESTIATO

The Moiazza appears at Forcella del Camp

across the bottom of Val dei Cantoni, affording magnificent views of the Civetta's fantastic soaring towers. In the opposite direction, across Val Cordevole appears elegant Monte Agner, its lofty point apparently floating over the tiny settlement of Listolade. A good way downhill from the turn-off for Van delle Sasse, is the key fork L (1430m, 30min) where AV1 heads S into beautiful wood on n.554. Accompanied by squirrels and masses of wildflowers, the path crosses a stream beneath Spiz della Mussaia then begins a steady climb through beech wood. Eroded gullies are crossed as the amazing west wall of the Moiazza is approached. A steep clamber brings you to

1hr 45min – Forcella Col dell'Orso (1823m), 'col of the bear', creatures hunted to extinction in these parts. A pause is in order to take in the inspiring sights S of the Pale di San Martino Altipiano, and closer at hand more Moiazza wonders.

Through springy dwarf pines, AV1 turns S across the head of wild isolated Busa del Camp. A short cable-aided passage helps you around an outcrop then it's mostly level walking. The rock faces feature an astounding range of precious blooms such as devil's claw and endemic bellflowers. The ruins of Casera del Camp precede a short climb to red clay **Forcella del Camp** (1933m, 45min) and the breathtaking spectacle of the Moiazza Sud and countless spires. Luckily, a matter of minutes down the other side, a bench at a crucifix lets you appreciate the line-up in comfort.

You now traverse E through larch wood alive with twittering finches and views to the rifugio on its wooded promontory, backed by another vision – the San Sebastiano-Tamer range, where AV1 ventures during the next stage. Proceeding across Van dei Cantoi you're joined by climbers returning from the renowned Ferrata Costantini, one of the longest and most difficult in the whole of the Dolomites. A final jaunt across scree and coloured earth leads to spanking brand new

1hr 35min – Rifugio Carestiato (1839m). ☎ 0437 62949, CAI, sleeps 30, open weekends early June then 20 June to 30 Sept, www.rifugiocarestiato.com.

> **Exit to Agordo (2hr 30min)**
> A handy, if long, route to Val Cordevole. Path n.548 entails a gentle but steady descent on a succession of paths, tracks, then minor road to the township of **Agordo** (611m) ⓘ 0437 62105, hotels, shops, buses (Dolomiti Bus) to Belluno as well as Alleghe and beyond.

STAGE 9
Rifugio Carestiato to Rifugio Pramperet

Time	4hr 20min
Distance	13km/8 miles
Ascent/Descent	550m/530m
Grade	2

A divine day's walking. It begins tracing the base of the eastern Moiazza before a road pass with accommodation and meals. AV1 then enters the realms of the Parco Nazionale delle Dolomiti Bellunesi, heading through quieter, less frequented places with the spectacular San Sebastiano-Tamer groups and beautiful woodland. A friendly rifugio, one of the few manned huts in this wild park, awaits at day's end.

From **Rifugio Carestiato** (1839m) a clear white gravel lane is followed E across pasture clearings and light wood. A path short cuts the last leg down to

40min – Passo Duran (1601m), at the foot of Cima Nord di San Sebastiano.

TREKKING IN THE DOLOMITES

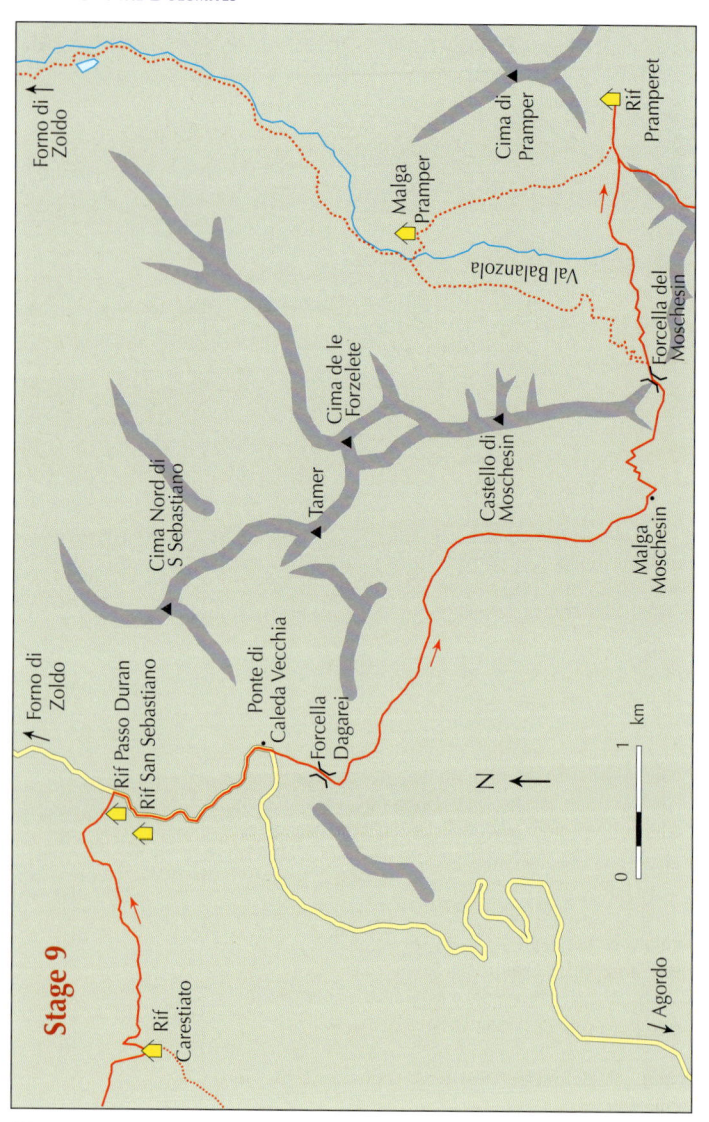

STAGE 9 – RIFUGIO CARESTIATO TO RIFUGIO PRAMPERET

San Sebastiano and Passo Duran

No bus services but two overnight options: **Rifugio Passo Duran** ☎ 0437 32034, private, sleeps 30, open weekends May and Oct, then June to Sept, accepts credit cards, www.rifugiopassoduran.it. Offering very reasonable rates and generous buffet breakfast, this basic alpine-style hut is run by an affable alpine guide who knows the Dolomites like the back of his hand.

Rifugio San Sebastiano ☎ 0437 62360, private, sleeps 25, open June to Oct, accepts credit cards, www.passoduran.it. The owner of this hotel has a wonderful collection of fossils from the area, starring black coral and megalodont shells. Dinner is served around an open fireplace.

AV1 proceeds downhill R (S) on the surfaced road for 2km, passing the turn-off for Malga Caleda (refreshments, meals). En route, an open outlook taking in the Vette Feltrine SW and the glacier-smoothed Pale di San Martino can be enjoyed. Where the road veers W to cross a stream is

20min – Ponte di Caleda Vecchia (1493m), car parking, picnic tables.

Here AV1/n.543 breaks off L (SW) near a signboard announcing the Parco Nazionale delle Dolomiti Bellunesi. Above due E is the yawning gully Van de Caleda separating San Sebastiano from the Tamer massif which now dominates the way. The going (S) gets steep, entering cool conifer forest that is soft underfoot thanks to pine needles, as you gain **Forcella Dagarei** (1620, 20min). Not long past an old hut the path emerges onto blinding white scree colonised by dwarf mountain pines, skirting the Tamer towers and chaotic rockfalls. The panorama is vast, even taking in the Cordevole valley and its villages.

AV1 proceeds effortlessly below Cima delle Forzelete before curving S dominated by imposing Castello di Moschesin. Wood of larch and pine shades walkers on the climb to **Malga Moschesin** (1800m) (drinking water, emergency shelter). A short climb E leads to a brilliant lookout at 1966m – ahead now are the Cime de Zita and Talvena. Coasting along the top of Val Clusa, the path reaches abandoned barracks at the ample saddle

2hr 30min – Forcella del Moschesin (1940m) in a veritable sea of mountain pines, alpenrose and bellflowers. The surrounding rocky realms conceal shy chamois, as well as shelters and tunnel systems dating back to both world wars.

Exit to Forno di Zoldo
If needs be, take path n.540 in descent N via Val Balanzola. Modernised dairy farm **Malga Pramper** (1540m, 30min) offers delicious home-made cakes, meals and a dorm for 8 ☎ 329 7862899. A shuttle bus (weekends July and Sept, daily Aug) runs to Forno di Zoldo. On foot allow 1hr as far as Pian de la Fopa and a further 1hr to Forno di Zoldo (868m) ⓘ 0437 787349, hotels, Dolomiti Bus to Longarone and trains.

AV1 keeps R for a modest rise with magnificent views N to the Zoldo valley backed by the Pelmo, Sorapiss and Antelao. Ahead NE is isolated Cima di Pramper.

STAGE 9 – RIFUGIO CARESTIATO TO RIFUGIO PRAMPERET

Heading E, descend a little to round Le Balanzole and down to join a lower path. The junction needed in Stage 10 is passed as you stroll towards the hut, which only appears at the last minute as it is surrounded by trees.

Long-abandoned barracks at Forcella del Moschesin

50min – Rifugio Pramperet aka Sommariva (1857m)
☎ 337 528403, CAI, sleeps 30, open 20 June to 20 Sept. Originally a simple herder's hut that offered a roof to adventurous walkers, it's still simple (plans were under way for a shower at the time of writing). The meals make up for lack of facilities as the cheery team here excel in soups, spicy meat stew and mouth-watering jam tarts.

Note Several steep exposed sections are encountered in Stage 10. Walkers who decide to give them a miss should bail out at this point: leave Rifugio Pramperet on path n.523 to Malga Pramper (30min) and follow the exit route to Forno di Zoldo given above.

STAGE 10
Rifugio Pramperet to Rifugio Pian de Fontana

Time	3hr
Distance	6.4km/4 miles
Ascent/Descent	540m/760m
Grade	2–3

One of the best stages on the whole of AV1, this deserves to be taken slowly to drink in the magnificent rugged scenery of the Dolomiti Bellunesi. Wildlife sightings are virtually guaranteed in this isolated ambience, far from civilisation. Superb wildflowers carpet the slopes, including many endemic species. In terms of difficulty, a clamber up an exposed ridge is encountered early on; not for the faint-hearted it is, thankfully, short. Further on, the final descent to Rifugio Pian de Fontana is pretty steep, and extra care is recommended. **Note** The widely used denomination 'Zita' encountered today is spelled 'Città' on older maps. The surrounds of Monte Talvena are a special reserve of great scientific interest and walkers are requested not to stray from marked paths. Many plants here are survivors from ice age 'islands' which harboured seeds from warmer climes. Examples are dwarf broom and mountain tragacanth, a type of milk vetch.

From **Rifugio Pramperet** (1857m) retrace your steps to the junction passed in Stage 9, and branch L (SW) on path n.514. A gentle climb ensues, the mountain pine vegetation giving way to thrift and saxifrage as things get stonier. Herds of chamois are at home on the slopes, as are marmots. A saddle, **Portela del Piazedel** (2097m) is the first of today's many lookout spots, this one taking in Castello di Moschesin and beyond to the Moiazza and Pale di San Martino. However, things improve fantastically as you proceed steadily S across inclined limestone slabs amidst rock jasmine and bevies of Rhaetian poppies. A final steep slog leads to a narrow, exciting ridge (2351m),

Walkers in a hurry to conclude AV1 may prefer to continue to Rifugio Bianchet, but be aware that it's a further 2hr 15min (Stage 11).

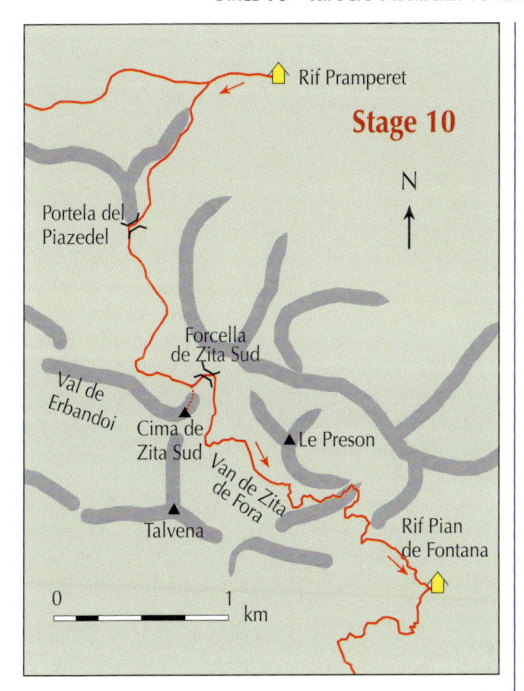

Stage 10 – Rifugio Pramperet to Rifugio Pian de Fontana

whose flanks plunge crazily to Val de Erbandoi. Around are immense stratified formations, notably Talvena, due S. Now for the short (20m) exposed climb up the near-vertical ridge E. It wastes no time in gaining broader grassy terraces where there is more space to admire the stunning panoramas. NW is Castello di Moschesin and, beyond, the spread of the Moiazza. It's not far at all around to

1hr 40min – Forcella de Zita Sud (2395m), the gateway to one of the most beautiful valleys on the whole of AV1: Van de Zita de Fora, scooped out by ancient glaciers and home to herds of chamois and colonies of playful marmots whose burrows pit the mountainsides. In the meantime, a highly recommended detour presents itself.

TREKKING IN THE DOLOMITES

> **Detour to Cime di Zita Sud (15min return)**
> Cairns mark the start of a faint path that sticks out R (S) up the inclined slab to **Cime di Zita Sud** (2450m) and wide-reaching views.

It's a gentle descent down alternating grass and grey scree slopes brightened by pink thrift blooms. All around are vast horizontal limestone tiers run through with grooves and rut channelling, the outcome of widespread karstification. Veering S you drop between the craggy Cima di Zita Sud (R) and a prominent ridge (L) culminating in Le Preson. The landscape is lunar, the frequent bowl-shaped hollows (*dolinas*) caused by the dissolving effect of rainwater, now harbouring wildflowers. Quiet, wild and wonderful. At the 2000m mark the path goes over a pronounced lip to traverse further E hugging rock faces studded with edelweiss and saxifrage. Abandoned shepherds' huts amidst dock and nettles are passed. To S the marvellous vision of the twin Schiara and Pelf is revealed, with the curious rock spike Gusela del Vescovà

The Schiara can be admired during the descent

(the 'bishop's needle), said to have provided anchorage for Noah's Ark – or St Martin's horse depending on the version. The rifugio comes into view but it's still a fair way down. The going (SE) becomes especially steep with loose stones underfoot – take extra care not to lose your footing. The last leg is flanked by a bright red outcrop, hence the name, as this is Val dei Ross.

1hr 20min – Rifugio Pian de Fontana (1632m). ☎ 335 6096819, CAI, sleeps 33, open 20 June to 20 Sept, www. goldnet.it/piandefontana. A clutch of nicely converted shepherds' huts, one of which serves as a cosy dining room with a roaring fire, the perfect setting for a dinner featuring steaming mounds of polenta smothered with melted local cheese or *Pastin* (a local sausage). ▶

> The hut's open setting makes it a good spot for observing birds of prey.

STAGE 11
Rifugio Pian de Fontana to La Pissa bus stop

Time	3hr 45min
Distance	13km/8 miles
Ascent/Descent	120m/1300m
Grade	2

This wonderful conclusion to AV1 crosses into wild Val Vescovà dominated by the giant Schiara, which rises to a giddy 2565m. The name is believed to derive from the Celtic for 'rings', once used as boundary markers. A fascinating story narrates that St Martin came this way and tied his horse to one of these rings, which turned into pure gold!

After Rifugio Bianchet, a fine place to stay the night before the return to 'civilisation', a dramatic ravine is descended on a well graded track, straightforward if long – 1300m height loss today! Beautiful, rugged surrounds and conclusion at La Pissa in Val Cordevole for the bus to Belluno. ▶

TREKKING IN THE DOLOMITES

> Those intent on concluding the AV1 with the spectacular via ferrata down the Schiara (variant route below) need to allow an extra day to reach Belluno. **Note** the alpine guide at **Rifugio 7° Alpini** can provide via ferrata kit and expert accompaniment (for a reasonable fee) for those who prefer not to be weighed down by kit.

At **Rifugio Pian de Fontana** (1632m) n.514 takes you SSW through beautiful beech wood, quickly losing 150m in height. At a stream (1490m, 15min) AV1 forks R for a testing, zigzagging climb out of Val dei Ross to ample

1hr – Forcella La Varetta (1701m). The Schiara rears up majestically at surprisingly close quarters now, hugely dominant, across thickly wooded Val Vescovà ('valley of the bishop'). The AV1 turns SE on an old herder's trail, a narrow but beautiful path cutting below Cime de la Scala, with plunging views. The rock flanks alongside

Signposting on the last leg

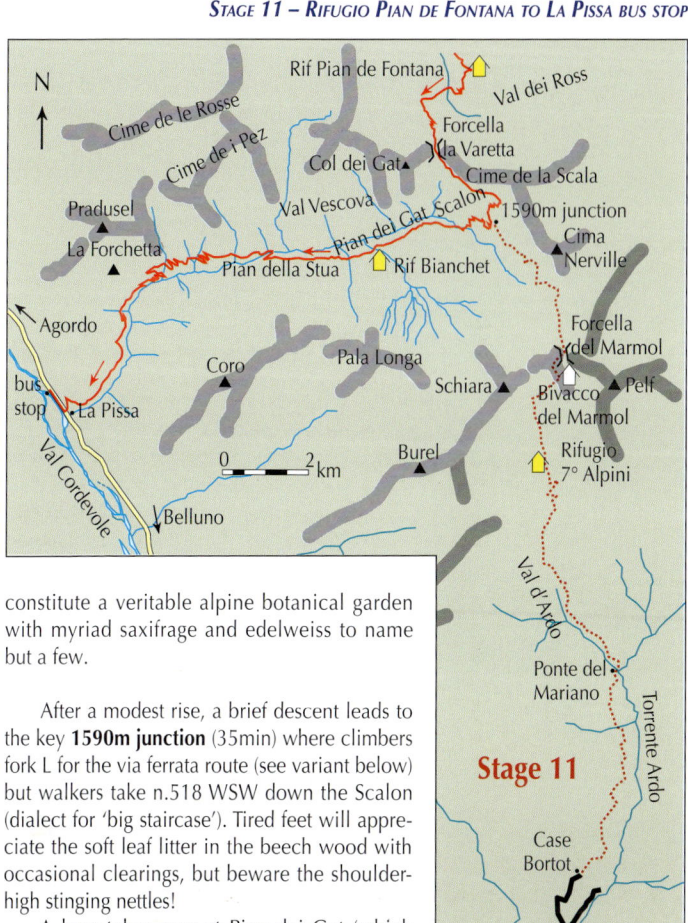

Stage 11 – Rifugio Pian de Fontana to La Pissa bus stop

constitute a veritable alpine botanical garden with myriad saxifrage and edelweiss to name but a few.

After a modest rise, a brief descent leads to the key **1590m junction** (35min) where climbers fork L for the via ferrata route (see variant below) but walkers take n.518 WSW down the Scalon (dialect for 'big staircase'). Tired feet will appreciate the soft leaf litter in the beech wood with occasional clearings, but beware the shoulder-high stinging nettles!

A lane takes over at Pian dei Gat (which derives from 'cloud' rather than an animal reference, as *gatto* is 'cat' in Italian), with thrilling Schiara views and

1hr 15min – Rifugio Bianchet (1245m). ☎ 0437 669226, CAI, sleeps 40, open June to Sept and weekends Apr, May and Oct, ivanicadore@alice.it.

Trekking in the Dolomites

A good gravel lane, used to supply the hut, leads easily W across Pian della Stua for a rapid succession of hairpin bends. Thick woods of conifers and sycamores flourish below towering cliffs that close in as you proceed. Ahead the wild Monti del Sole appear above the treetops.

The track sticks to the R side of the ravine, its L side precipitous grey flanks. As the ravine opens a little the Val Cordevole floor comes into sight and the track bears R (leading to Pinei and a bus stop, marginally longer) but the AV1 takes the path breaking off L. A little slippery due to exposed tree roots, it drops quickly to a footbridge over a gaping chasm, and water pool and cascade, then steps to the roadside at

1hr 30min – La Pissa (448m). Turn R past the car park for the bus stop on the opposite side of the road near a derelict house. The last couple of refuges on AV1 display the relevant timetables so try to time your arrival with a Dolomiti Bus, as there's nowhere nice to wait, or any shelter for that matter. **Note** 2.5km away (S) is La Stanga with a nice café-restaurant where tickets are sold, but it means risking your life as cars speed by on this trafficked road. Buy your ticket on board, with a small surcharge unless you somehow managed to purchase one beforehand.

It's a 20min bus trip to the pleasant alpine town of **Belluno** (370m), derived from the Celtic for 'splendid hill'; its backdrop is the sheer S face of the Schiara.

Via ferrata variant
Intending climbers **must** be suitably experienced and equipped and be aware that both misty conditions and icy stretches are commonly encountered. **Note**: Bivacco del Marmol is currently unusable due to damage from heavy 2010 snowfalls.

From the **1590m junction** path n.514 heads off SE amidst thick vegetation. Old herder's hut Casonet di Nerville (1641m, emergency shelter only) is soon passed as you climb out of the trees along the edge of the valley towards the great ridge that brings together the Schiara and the Pelf.

Stage 11 – Rifugio Pian de Fontana to La Pissa bus stop

The going becomes rougher over slabs, scree and snow patches; the way not always clear on the slog S up a gully to

2h 30min – Forcella del Marmol (2262m), an airy spot where the via ferrata itself begins.

Ignore the route E for the Pelf summit, and carefully follow paint splashes for the clamber R (SW). This proceeds over wet rock slabs to 2350m to round a spur, disregarding a route for the Schiara summit that forks off W. Now a long tricky series of cable-aided climbs leads down to a little rock terrace where the unmanned dark red metal cabin stands

20min – Bivacco del Marmol (2266m), sleeps 9.

The Ferrata Marmol continues SW along ledges, across deep gullies and down ladders with lengthy exposure. A small cave with a possible water supply is touched on.
Ignore the branch W for Via Ferrata Zacchi (n.503) and, 100m below at the foot of the cliff, at the monumental Porton ravine 'gateway' at 1780m, your feet will be back on grassy ground for the final straightforward (albeit steep) path to

3hr – Rifugio 7° Alpini (1502m) ☎ 0437 941631, CAI, sleeps 60, open mid-June to late Sept, www.rifugiosettimoalpini.it. The hut was named *Settimo Alpini* for an alpine battalion. It is set against an inspirational amphitheatre of rock walls, an attractive playground for climbers and via ferrata enthusiasts.

A lovely, if long and knee-knocking, descent on a good path n.501 follows S along the *calvario*. Cool wood fills the Val d'Ardo where a crystal clear mountain stream runs. After the third bridge crossing, at **Ponte del Mariano (681m)**, AV1 takes a lane that ascends a little to the tiny hamlet of

2hr – Case Bortot (694m) with a lovely café/restaurant.

From here it's surfaced road for 3km to

45min – Bolzano Bellunese (541m) where a Dolomiti Bus can be caught the rest of the way to Belluno.

Drop in to the Tourist Office (Piazza Duomo 2 ⓘ 0437 940083) to be awarded with your well-earned

TREKKING IN THE DOLOMITES

The bus stop at La Pissa

AV1 badge on presentation of the rifugi stamps collected en route.

It is a good transport hub with trains to Calalzo and ongoing buses for Cortina thence Dobbiaco and Lago di Braies, otherwise the rail services S to Venice.

Accommodation possibilities include centrally located Albergo delle Alpi ☎ 0437 940545, www.dellealpi.it or B&B La Cerva ☎ 0437 944179, www.lacerva.it.

ALTA VIA 2

View over upper Val Badia from path to Passo Poma (AV2 Stage 2)

Trekking in the Dolomites

INTRODUCTION

An elegant Tyrolean town with a long history as bishop's see, Bressanone/Brixen is a marvellous starting point for the superb Alta Via 2 (AV2) long-distance traverse of the Dolomites. Standing at the confluence of the Rienza and Isarco rivers, whose waters blend with the mighty

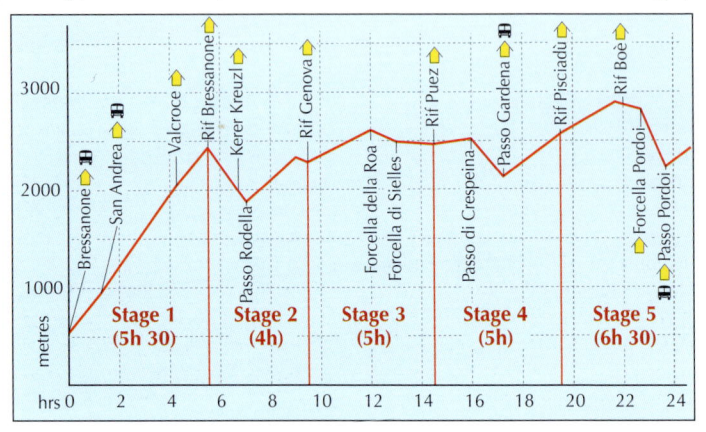

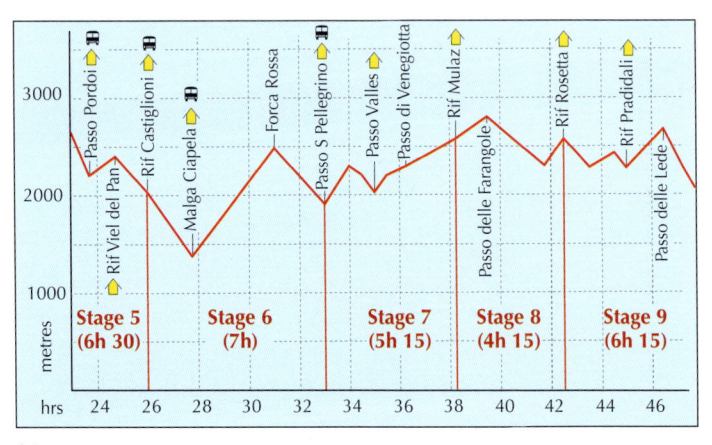

94

Rifugio Boè on the Sella lunar upland (Stage 5)

Adige further south, it is convenient to reach from either Austria or northern Italy by rail or road. The charming traffic-free centre is worth a wandering visit for its porticoed streets, and its Gothic and Baroque architecture – including the 18th century cathedral with its soaring spire. Bressanone's Palazzo Vescovile (bishops' residence) boasts a delightful collection of traditional Christmas cribs and nativity scenes, with ornate figures hundreds of years old. The town also happens to be an excellent place to go shopping and stock up on food at the open-air markets, inviting bakeries, delis and supermarkets. Apart from the first village on the way up, San Andrea, this is your only chance to do so until Malga Ciapela in Stage 6.

In addition to a helpful Tourist Office ⓘ 0472 836401, it has a vast range of hotel accommodation as well as a centrally located Youth Hostel ☎ 0472 279999, www.bressanone.jugendherberge.it.

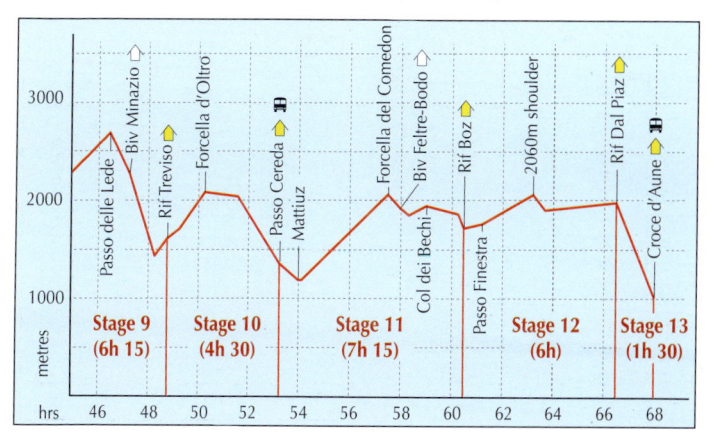

TREKKING IN THE DOLOMITES

Bressanone
5h 30min
Rif Bressanone
4h
Rif Genova
5h
Rif Puez
5h
Rif Pisciadù
6h 30min
Rif Castiglioni
7h
Passo S Pellegrino
5h 15min
Rif Mulaz
4h 15min
Rif Rosetta
6h 15min
Rif Treviso
4h 30min
Passo Cereda
7h 15min
Rif Boz
6h
Rif Dal Piaz
1h 30min
Croce d'Aune

Alta Via 2

Bressanone 561m
Rif Città di Bressanone 2446m
Rif Genova 2297m
Rif Puez 2475m
Passo Gardena 2137m
Corvara
Rif Pisciadù 2587m
Rif Boè 2873m
Sella
Passo Pordoi 2239m
Rif Castiglioni 2050m
Malga Ciapela 1384m
Marmolada
Passo S Pellegrino 1919m
Moena
Cencenighe
Passo Valles 2031m
Falcade
Rif Mulaz 2571m
Agordo
Pale di S Martino
S Martino di Castrozza
Biv Minazio 2295m
Rif Rosetta 2581m
Rif Treviso 1631m
Rif Pradidali 2278m
Passo Cereda 1360m
Fiera di Primiero
Biv Feltre-Bodo 1930m
Rif Boz 1718m
Vette Feltrine
Rif Dal Piaz 1993m
Croce d'Aune 1015m
Feltre 325m

N ↑

0 — 10 km

96

STAGE 1
Bressanone to Rifugio Città di Bressanone

Time	5hr 30min
Distance	11km/6.8 miles
Ascent	1900m
Grade	2

Starting out from valley level, AV2 makes its way through farming villages to higher spectacular reaches well away from the hustle and bustle. The destination is the Plose, a nondescript mountain well known to winter skiers and mountain bikers, but (of greater interest to AV2 walkers) host to a superbly appointed rifugio. It's a perfect first night out on the trek, as isolated from the main Dolomites it offers unrivalled views onto their northwestern faces, which actually start here. A brilliant start.

A short stretch along tarmac gives way to lovely paths and meadows, then forest for a long, long climb – which can, nonetheless, be shortened. In fact non-purists will appreciate the buses and lift to ease the 1900m height gain demanded by this opening stage: SAD buses from the railway station run to San Andrea and the departure station of the Plose *Seilbahn* (gondola car) that whisks you up to Valcroce; the summer operating period running from mid-June to early October.

From Valcroce you are in open heath land, where panoramas are non-stop through 360°. Generally speaking no particular difficulty is encountered, but the massive height gain should not be under-rated.

A final variant cutting out Plose altogether makes use of the bus from Bressanone via San Andrea and Plancios, thence Skihütte (see Stage 2).

From the railway station at **Bressanone** (561m), the street Mozartallee leads due E across the grey-green Isarco to a T intersection where you fork R, signed for Plose. (If you detour by way of the town centre, from the main square head E for the river and a minor bridge, then turn R to reach this spot – allow an extra 30min). After

Bressanone

10min S along the road, branch L on n.4A at a fountain on Kirchsteig. This becomes a country lane to a lovely old manor house dating back to the 1200s. Red/white stripes guide you through apple orchards and past the old church (S Maria in Sand, 620m). Then it's L across a stream and the final stretch of tarmac to where a path (n.4A) veers sharp L up through chestnut and pine wood, then fields and farms. The road is joined briefly as you approach

1hr 15min – San Andrea (961m). SAD buses, hotels, groceries ⓘ 0472 850008.

On the corner of the Gasthof Gasserhof and its inviting beer garden, turn uphill on n.4, which threads its way past houses old and new, all bright with window boxes spilling geraniums. A final wander through wood brings you to the **Plose lift departure station and bus stop** (1057m, 15min) and a difficult decision – to walk or to ride...

Behind the restaurant building a narrow surfaced lane is the start of n.17 for Valcroce. It quickly becomes

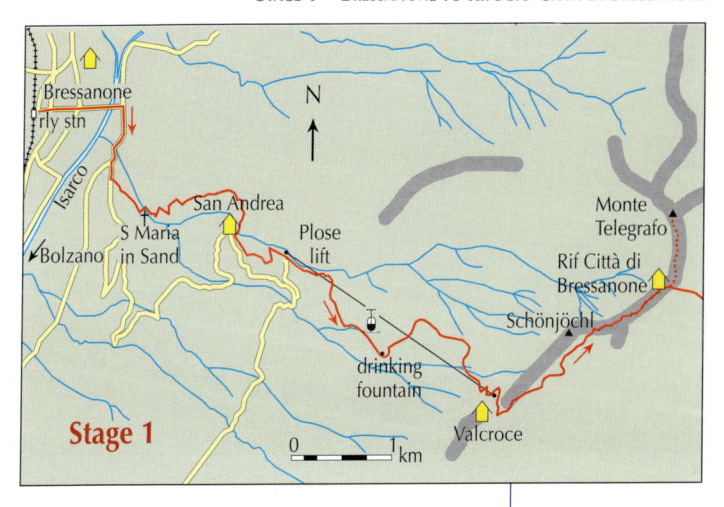

STAGE 1 – BRESSANONE TO RIFUGIO CITTÀ DI BRESSANONE

a clear, if narrow, path climbing steadily through conifer wood with carpets of bilberry shrubs. Logging means bare patches where trees are cleared but the way is usually well signed at the many forks with intersecting forestry tracks and ski slopes. After a stretch SE below the gondola lift cables, at a **drinking fountain** at 1450m it forks decidedly L (NE). Little-frequented n.17 now embarks on a relentless, and a tad monotonous, zigzagging climb through woodland with the odd rough section. Finally, some 600m higher up, it emerges at

3hr – Valcroce/Kreuztal (2050m) and the gondola car arrival station. Only metres away is beautifully placed café-restaurant-guesthouse Pension Geisler ☎ 0472 521319 sleeps 25, open end May to mid-Oct, www.pension-geisler.com.

Path n.7 heads NE for the straightforward climb past ski lifts and pistes through shrubby vegetation of heather and cowberries, with cows and sheep at pasture. Keeping R under Schönjöchl it reaches a saddle with bird's-eye views over Bressanone and the valley N towards the

TREKKING IN THE DOLOMITES

Rifugio Città di Bressanone and the Odle di Eores from Monte Telegrafo

Brenner Pass. After a wooden cross the white refuge building is only a few more vertical minutes away.

1hr 15min – Rifugio Città di Bressanone (2446m). ☎ 0472 521333, CAI, sleeps 60, open early June to late Oct, accepts credit cards, www.plosehuette.com. Modern bar/restaurant designed for winter skiers, but summer guests are fed well and get to stay in cosy timber-lined sleeping quarters.

There is a magnificent outlook here to the jagged spectacular barrier of the Odle di Eores (slightly ahead of the main Odle needles, which soar higher), then SE is twin-peaked Sass de Putia; SW rises Sassolungo flanked by the Sciliar massif. Quite amazing!

Side trip to Monte Telegrafo (20min return)
The Austrian Tyrol line-up of peaks is better admired from 2486m Monte Telegrafo, the neighbouring mound sprouting a clutter of aerials. A helpful *Rundpanoramatisch* (orientation table) identifies all those rocky points through 360°.

STAGE 2
Rifugio Città di Bressanone to Rifugio Genova

Time	4hr
Distance	13km/8 miles
Ascent/Descent	610m/760m
Grade	2

A magnificent stage with straightforward walking and breathtaking views. Once the ski zone of Plose is left behind, woodland with a wealth of elegant Arolla pine is traversed. From a road, AV2 enters the Parco Naturale Puez-Odle, climbing over scree and fallen rock to a pass and pasture upland where the destination hut stands, a comfortable place serving traditional Südtirol fare. A couple of café-restaurants are touched on today, lovely spots for a drink, meal or overnight stay.

The relative brevity of this stage – 4hr – means you can take it easy. On the other hand, if you have time, there is a highly recommended optional 2hr ascent of 2875m Sass de Putia. The northernmost Dolomite, it boasts record-making views to 449 church spires across the Südtirol, but binoculars are a help – see below.

Leave **Rifugio Città di Bressanone** (2446m) L on n.4, which follows a fence with a stunning outlook N to the snowbound Italo-Austrian border. In gentle descent it passes two ski lifts, then changes direction abruptly a couple of times, heading essentially S over grassy slopes. It cuts across a dirt road and heads into Arolla wood, run through with trickling streams and thick with banks of alpenrose and bilberry shrubs.

Several lengths of guiding cable accompany a stretch (no exposure) cut into the mountainside and over a footbridge. This emerges on meadows dotted with photogenic timber chalets and soon joins a dirt road (turn L) close to

TREKKING IN THE DOLOMITES

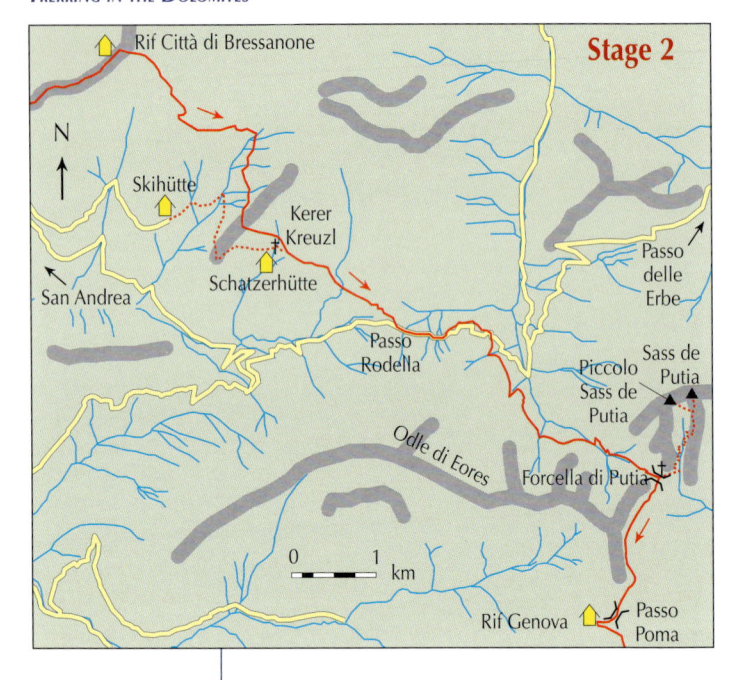

1hr 10min – Kerer Kreuzl (2000m) with an artistic wood crucifix. A short cut from Skihütte slots in here.

> **Variant access from Skihütte (30min)**
> From Skihütte aka Plancios di Dentro (1890m), walk past the hotels and restaurants E along the road (n.8), which soon becomes a broad forestry track. It crosses a stream and climbs gently above the tree line to the Karer Kreuzl junction.

Close by is charming **Schatzerhütte** ☎ 0472 521343, open May to Nov, www.schatzerhuette.com.
With a wonderful view to towering Sass de Putia SE, not far along n.4 branches R (SE) through wood, bypassing eatery *Enzianhütte*. In sight of the road, ignore a

STAGE 2 – RIFUGIO CITTÀ DI BRESSANONE TO RIFUGIO GENOVA

turn-off and keep L for boardwalks across marshy terrain to the road at

20min – Passo Rodella aka Halsl (1886m) and Rodelalm farm-cum-café. This is the divider between the Plose and the Putia groups.

Ahead, beneath looming Sass de Putia is Passo delle Erbe, which provides access to Val Badia. Only minutes along the tarmac n.4 drops L to avoid the traffic, keeping parallel to the road for a short spell and rejoining it close to the key fork R. Here, AV2 enters the Puez-Odle park. Constantly SSE a good path coasts through wood and over a stream beneath the impressive **Odle di Eores** – glance up and the significance of the ancient Ladin term 'Odle' or 'needles' will start sinking in.

As the path enters the gully leading to Forcella di Putia, it begins climbing relentlessly SE over broken rock and cascading watercourses. This is AV2's first taste of being dwarfed by awesome Dolomite landscapes, as above is the W face of Sass de Putia, whose

At Forcella di Putia

TREKKING IN THE DOLOMITES

lower layers are a fascinating lesson in geology. Several paths join up and you move to the L side at a huge boulder. Zigzags with timber reinforcements help the climb, but they may be buried as snow lies late here. You finally emerge at

2hr – Forcella di Putia (2357m) and a crucifix, not to mention dramatic contrast of vast pastureland and a gorgeous outlook E to Sasso della Croce and Cunturines over Val Badia, and even Lagazuoi and the Pelmo, visited on AV1. Ahead S is the many-turreted Puez-Odle massif, tomorrow's destination.

Ascent of Sass de Putia (2hr return)
Sharp L from **Forcella di Putia** is the path leading into the central fold of Sass de Putia, where a shallow gully-valley often harbours late-lying snow. Wide curves climb steadily – keep R at a fork for a brief crest passage to a broad saddle at 2760m. Here, tackle the final cable-aided stretch via an exposed shoulder and hands-on climb to the 2875m summit of **Sass de Putia**. Should that not appeal, turn L (W) at the saddle for the easy route to the twin peak, **Piccolo Sass de Putia**, only metres lower. The views are quite amazing and range 360°, taking in a vast selection of Dolomites along with the northern snow-capped Austrian Alps. Tame alpine choughs keep you company. Return the same way to **Forcella di Putia**.

Now, a mostly level path heads off S over grassy flowered slopes with magnificent views, to **Passo Poma** (2340m). Only a short flight of steps R is

30min – Rifugio Genova aka Schlütterhütte (2297m).
☎ 0472 840132, CAI, sleeps 90, open mid-June to mid-Oct, www.schlueterhuette.com. A lovely, rambling timber building inaugurated in 1898, it was constructed by a councillor from Dresden and donated to the DÖAV, the Austro-German Alpine Club. In 1925, when the region was transferred to Italian government, it was taken over by the Genoese branch of CAI, the Italian club, and subsequently the Bressanone section in the aftermath of

Rifugio Genova interior

the Second World War. Lively, popular place run by an extended family from the area.

STAGE 3
Rifugio Genova to Rifugio Puez

Time	5hr
Distance	12km/7.5 miles
Ascent/Descent	820m/645m
Grade	2–3

A spectacular long traverse with brilliant views all day. After contouring flowered pasture slopes comes a fatiguing climb, followed by a long series of more ups and downs – and a short aided stretch. As a fitting reward you will venture onto the unworldly Puez plateau. This vast undulating *altopiano* is sparse in vegetation but rich in fossils, such as ammonites and megalodont shells. The upper rock layer has eroded into bizarre monumental ▶

'sculptures'. The area can be crossed safely now, and this brilliant stage is brought to its close at a friendly family-run hut.

A lower altitude – and longer – variant puts you in a position to admire the magnificent Odle rock spires from their 'best' northern side. (The name means 'needle' in Ladin). This is courtesy of the splendid, renowned Adolf Munkel Weg trail, which was created in 1904–5 and named after the founder of the Dresden branch of the German Alpine Club. Afterwards comes a stiff climb to meadows, then the variant rejoins the main AV2 route just before Forcella di Sielles. It can easily be broken into two stages thanks to handy refuges – see below.

Both main route and variant have a tricky (albeit short) stretch.

From **Rifugio Genova** (2297m), n.3 strikes out uphill SE at first to cut around Bronsoi over flowered slopes. A stretch due S leads to an amazingly panoramic col at 2421m where the Puez group rears ahead, not to mention the Seceda giant and the elegant Odle needles.

Veering SW it ambles past marmot colonies and detours briefly via Medalares Alm (2293m), to reach **Kreuzjoch** (2293m), and an exit path to Longiarù in Val Badia.

Approaching the Odle rock faces and Piz Duleda, the path proceeds due S over vast wooded valley head dominated by scree flows. Dodging a couple of outcrops it moves onto scree base for interminable zigzags and a good chance of late-lying snow to gain

2hr 30min – Forcella della Roa (2617m) a broad saddle frequented by hungry alpine choughs. The brilliant outlook takes in Sass Putia and the Italo-Austrian border, as well as tempting glimpses of the Sella and even Piz Boè.

It's an easy descent into a chaotic amphitheatre. Take care not to miss the fork L where AV2 departs ways from n.3 (which continues for Rifugio Firenze). The clear path picks its way across fallen shattered rocks and yellow poppies to where it links with n.2 (from Rifugio Firenze and the variant). It's a puff-inducing climb E to

STAGE 3 – RIFUGIO GENOVA TO RIFUGIO PUEZ

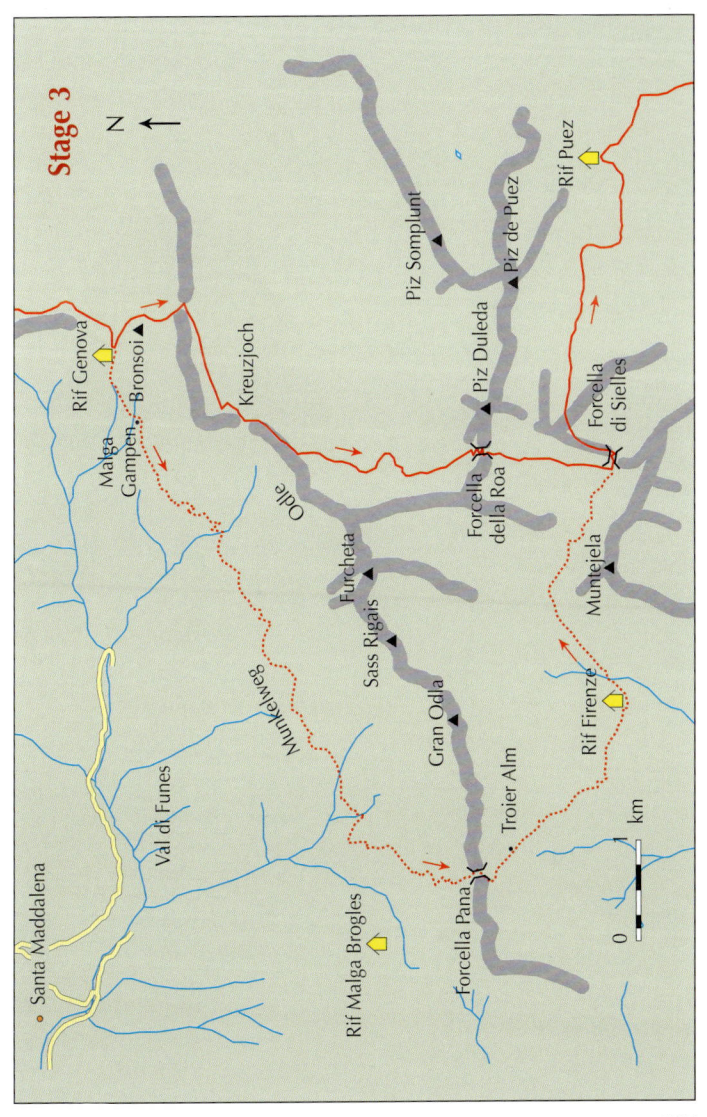

*Aided stretch after
Forcella di Sielles*

STAGE 3 – RIFUGIO GENOVA TO RIFUGIO PUEZ

1hr – Forcella di Sielles (2505m), above spectacular steep-sided Vallunga with its glacially sculpted U shape, and the vast Puez plateau. Edelweiss abound here.

Cable-aided stretches with a little exposure climb the crest N, reaching 2590m, then a narrow scree path leads onto ample grassy slopes with views to the Civetta, Pelmo, Antelao and the Tofane.

Veering E, the path meanders over pasture enjoyed by sheep and basins bright with a riot of rock campion and forget-me-not. Past an exit route for Santa Cristina at the head of the mighty Vallunga, a gentle uphill stretch continues to the hut, visible only at the very last moment.

1hr 30min – Rifugio Puez (2475m) ☎ 0471 795365, CAI, sleeps 90, open 15 June to 15 Oct. The refuge's isolated situation, far from jeep tracks and lacking the usual mechanised cableway, means supplies have to be brought in by costly helicopter. Clean and efficient establishment, with delicious strudel and luscious hot chocolate, but rather cramped sleeping quarters.

Rifugio Malga Brogles and the magnificent Odle (see variant on p. 110)

The Odle variant

From **Rifugio Genova** (2297m), path n.35 heads W down flowered slopes to Malga Gampen (2062m, drinks and meals). It joins the jeep track SW through wood to where the Rio San Zenon watercourse is crossed at 1868m (40min). Forking SW off the track is n.35, the start of the justifiably popular Munkelweg or Sentiero delle Odle. Gentle meandering ups and downs past the foot of awesome scree flows and soaring elegant rock turrets follow, not to mention a wealth of fossils and brilliant wild blooms.

Ignore the numerous turn-offs R to inviting farms-cum-summer eateries, however tempting they may be! Not long after junctions for Forcella Mesdì and Funes, is a signed fork L (1hr 30min) for path n.6 to Forcella Pana.

(Should you have a raging desire to enjoy a memorable sunset on the Odle, then continue on n.35 for 30min to old fashioned dairy farm alias **Rifugio Malga Brogles** (2045m) cell ☎ 338 4600101, sleeps 20 in dorm and rooms, open July to Sept, no shower. Another path departs from here for Forcella Pana.)

You climb initially S past huge boulders to zigzag up steep scree, gradually tending W towards the narrow pass, hidden from view until the last leg. A final chimney aided with cables and timber traverses leads to

3hr 40min – Forcella Pana (2447m). You emerge in a different world of rolling meadows and chalets, and vast views across Val Gardena to the Sella and other giants. (Close by is the Seceda and cable-car to the resort of Ortisei in Val Gardena.) Take path n.1 for the stroll SE past newly rebuilt **Troier Alm** (2271m) offering meals and drinks. In gentle descent across Alpe di Cisles is

45min – Rifugio Firenze (2037m). ☎ 0471 796307, CAI, sleeps 90, open June to mid-Oct, www.rifugiofirenze.com. From here the smart resort of Santa Cristina (ⓘ 0471 777800) can be reached on foot or by lift.

In the shade of Sass Rigais and its Odle neighbours, path n.2 heads NE climbing across terrain with sparse greenery, rounding Muntejela and veering R (SSE). Entering a stern stone amphitheatre it puffs up to

1hr 30min – where the main AV2 route from Forcella della Roa slots in.

STAGE 4
Rifugio Puez to Rifugio Pisciadù

Time	5hr
Distance	9km/6 miles
Ascent/Descent	660m/550m
Grade	3

Today's opener is a delightful meander that continues across the wonderful Puez plateau. The pretty lakes dotting its surface were a source of fear in olden times as dragons reportedly slumbered in their depths! Then comes a descent to one of the most beautiful Dolomite road passes, Passo Gardena. Connecting Ladin-speaking Val Gardena and Val Badia it has the bonus of hotels and buses, but for walkers on the AV2 it represents the gateway to the Sella group: a unique, awe-inspiring massif akin to a fortress that stands isolated. Its sheer forbidding flanks and terraces are recognisable from afar.

A dramatic gully slices deep into the block, entailing hands-on clambering and cable-aided passages – this earns the stage its grade 3 difficulty. It all concludes with an overnight stay at a rifugio on a superb high altitude platform. **Note** It's inadvisable to embark on the ascent to Rifugio Pisciadù late in the day in unsettled weather; even in good conditions you can expect to encounter vast numbers of climbers descending Val Setus on their return from vie ferrate.

From **Rifugio Puez** (2475m), well-trodden n.2 passes the hut's flag pole and skirts the head of Vallunga where views extend SW to the Sciliar. It continues across the fascinating altopiano embedded with fossils and dotted with curious volcano-like mounds. Needless to say the outlook is vast. After a stretch S looking towards the Sassongher peak, it passes through a short gully with timber reinforcement, veering sharp R past **Forcella di Ciampai** (2366m, exit path for Colfosco). Keep straight on (SW), dipping through grassy basins and across streams

Trekking in the Dolomites

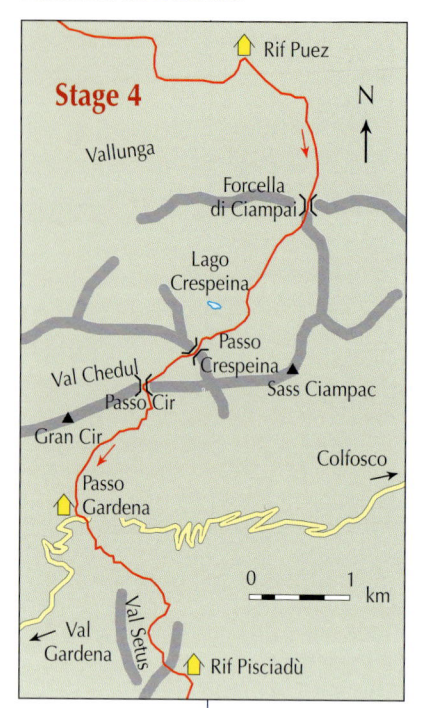

not far from the green water of Lago Crespeina, an inviting picnic spot. Beneath Sass Ciampac zigzags lead up to

1hr 30min – Passo Crespeina (2528m) and its artistic crucifix. Good place to contemplate the altopiano for the last time.

With a decent view to Sassolungo SW, the path descends steeply into the head of Val Chedul, ignores a path for Selva and crawls L over broken rubble to **Passo Cir** (2469m) where weird and wonderful rock spires and eroded formations reminiscent of totem poles abound. You meander into a bowl full of pinnacles, soon emerging from this rock jungle to awesome views of the Sella, close at hand now. The path continues through dwarf mountain pines and past the chalet eatery Jimmy's Hütte in the shade of the Gran Cir to a gravel track which concludes at the road and

1hr 15min – Passo Gardena (2137m). Hotel Cir ☎ 0471 795127, www.hotelcir.com or Rifugio Berghaus Frara ☎ 0471 795225, sleeps 40 in dorm and rooms, open late June to end Sept, credit cards accepted, www.rifugiofrara. it. SAD buses run down both sides of the pass, namely E to Colfosco in Val Badia as well as W to Val Gardena resorts.

However, tarry not as a stiff climb still awaits walkers intent on finishing this stage today.

Alongside Berghaus Frara path n.666 climbs straight up a grass-earth crest then bears L (SE) through shrubby

STAGE 4 – RIFUGIO PUEZ TO RIFUGIO PISCIADÙ

vegetation at the foot of soaring cliffs. After half an hour the yawning mouth to wild Val Setus is reached. (The name derives from 'haymaker', for the lush meadows below). AV2 forks R (S) for the steep assault up this awesome ravine of mobile scree and stone rubble, often harbouring snow well into summer. With the sound of traffic on the snaking road gradually dimming below, well-marked regular curves ascend steadily keeping to the right-hand side – out of the way of the odd rock fall from higher chutes. A fair way up, the path veers L across a gully for an aided stretch fitted with iron rungs, spikes and a thick cable attached firmly to the rock face. Exposure is medium and there are plentiful footholds, but it will take around half an hour before you emerge onto a spectacular 2610m terrace beneath Sass da Lech. Branch L for the short stroll to

2hr 15min – Rifugio Pisciadù (2587m) aka Rifugio Franco Cavazza ☎ 0471 836292, CAI, sleeps 104, open beg. July to end Sept. This very pleasant, modern, roomy hut is well run and occupies a breathtaking platform, from which the township of Colfosco can be seen far below.

Passo Gardena and the Sella

113

Rifugio Pisciadù and its lake

The nearby tarn Lago di Pisciadù supplies both the refuge and a nearby waterfall, which gave its name to many landforms here. Bathing is – understandably – forbidden!

STAGE 5
Rifugio Pisciadù to Rifugio Castiglioni

Time	6hr 30min
Distance	14.5km/9 miles
Ascent/Descent	710m/1250m
Grade	3

This is an awesome stage, which covers incredibly varied landscapes – ranging from the stark Sella to the lush flowered slopes of volcanic origin on the historic Viel del Pan, and to the immense glaciated Marmolada.

STAGE 5 – RIFUGIO PISCIADÙ TO RIFUGIO CASTIGLIONI

First off today AV2 climbs further up the terraces of the majestic Sella to a vast lunar upland inhabited by ibex and choughs. Cairns, pole markers and red arrows painted on the ground show the way to a welcoming rifugio. Here an optional ascent of popular walker's peak Piz Boè is on the cards; at 3152m it is simply spectacular. Then it's a plunge (or cable-car) to a strategic road pass where hotels and exit buses can be had. Thereafter is an easy path with brilliant views of the 3342m Marmolada, the highest mountain in the Dolomites. Geological interest is high as this is a vast volcanic intrusion, and so, naturally, is flora. This so-called *Viel del Pan* ('way of bread') was once used by grain smugglers to avoid hefty taxes imposed by the Venetian Republic. Restored in the late 1800s, it is also known as the *Bindelweg* after a former president of the DÖAV. After a short drop to a manmade lake, the day concludes at a historic refuge.

From **Rifugio Pisciadù** (2587m), signposts for n.666 point you S skirting the lake.

The path climbs slowly S cutting across scree falls from the yellowish W flank of Cima Pisciadù. A fork L avoids a short aided rock passage (signed *attrezzato*), and you climb into debris-filled Val di Tita where snow patches inevitably abound. In a squelchy hollow you pass the turn-off for Cima Pisciadù. Keep R for more gentle climbing via a narrow gully to a rough platform where a detour to the edge gives an airy view back to the refuge and its lake. Up at the 2900m mark is level terrain and sweeping views over the vast Altipiano delle Meisules, a stone desert where ibex surprisingly find enough summer sustenance to thrive. Elegant rounded Sass Pordoi with its sheer sides is virtually straight ahead; the arrival station of the cable-car from Passo Pordoi perched on its peak. S is Piz Boè, a repeater and hut clinging tight.

Next is an easy descent to a flat zone and signed path junction for Val Lasties, long believed to be the dwelling place of witches. Nearby L, in the proximity of Torre Berger, you get your first unnervingly dramatic glimpses down plunging Val di Mesdì. An ensuing

> Thanks to the string of refuges en route, this rather lengthy day can always be split into less tiring chunks if so desired.

TREKKING IN THE DOLOMITES

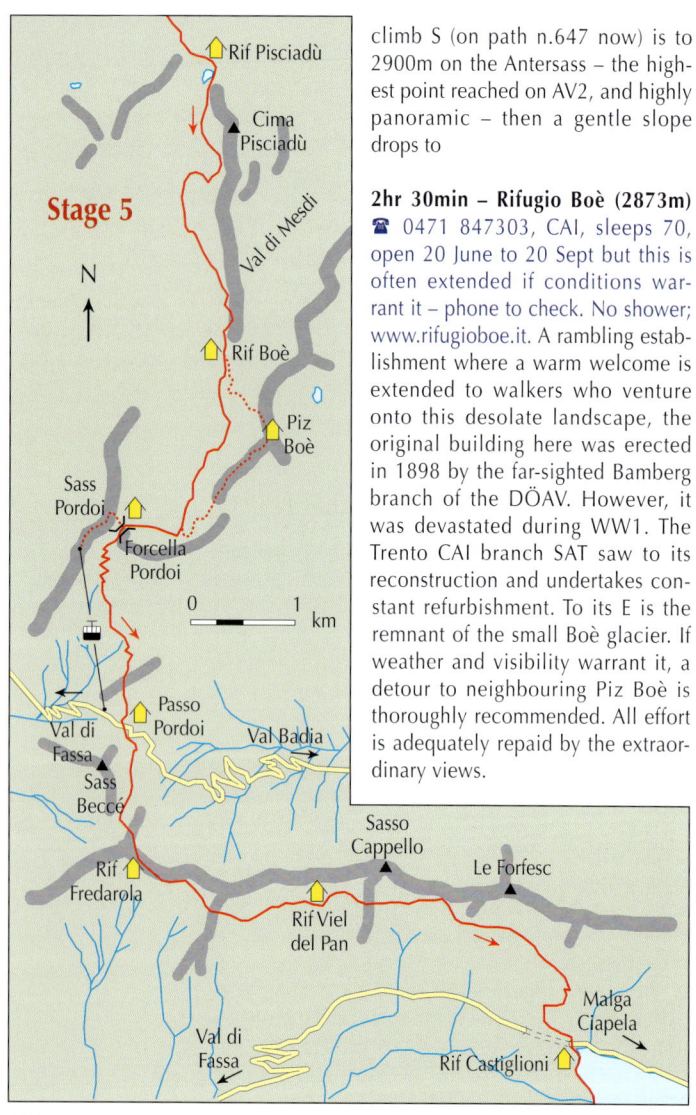

climb S (on path n.647 now) is to 2900m on the Antersass – the highest point reached on AV2, and highly panoramic – then a gentle slope drops to

2hr 30min – Rifugio Boè (2873m)
☎ 0471 847303, CAI, sleeps 70, open 20 June to 20 Sept but this is often extended if conditions warrant it – phone to check. No shower; www.rifugioboe.it. A rambling establishment where a warm welcome is extended to walkers who venture onto this desolate landscape, the original building here was erected in 1898 by the far-sighted Bamberg branch of the DÖAV. However, it was devastated during WW1. The Trento CAI branch SAT saw to its reconstruction and undertakes constant refurbishment. To its E is the remnant of the small Boè glacier. If weather and visibility warrant it, a detour to neighbouring Piz Boè is thoroughly recommended. All effort is adequately repaid by the extraordinary views.

STAGE 5 – RIFUGIO PISCIADÙ TO RIFUGIO CASTIGLIONI

> **Variant via Piz Boè**
> Path n.638 heads uphill mostly SE, making its way across scree. It heads for a prominent bastion and a lengthy aided stretch, which can prove difficult in icy conditions. The crest of awe-inspiring **Piz Boè** (3152m, 1hr) hosts a repeater and wooden hut Capanna Fassa (3152m) (meals and even accommodation ☎ 0462 601723, sleeps 20, open 20 June to 20 Sept). Out with the map and compass to identify those extraordinary mountain ranges visible every way you look.
> A little easier than the ascent, the descent route n.638 follows a ridge SW, scrambling down the outward corner. At its base a clear path continues in the same direction to join the main AV2 route from Rifugio Boè.

Heading S across the undulating rock upland, path n.627 crosses well-trodden snow patches. It cuts across scree flows from Piz Boè, including curiously red boulders. Cairns, poles and waymarks need to be followed carefully across undulating terrain to where a series of ledges feature fossilised shells. The path from Piz Boè links in for the final leg coasting W to

40min – Forcella Pordoi (2829m) and dauntingly positioned Rifugio Forcella Pordoi c/o ☎ 0462 767500 or ☎ cell 368 3557505 (**Note** phone signal not guaranteed), open mid-June to end Sept, sleeps 25 in dorm and rooms. It took over 500 helicopter trips to transport the material needed for this chalet! Great place to stay.

> For more views (had enough yet?) or a restful cable-car trip down to Passo Pordoi, climb on the wide path above the building for a final 100m uphill to the marvellous belvedere and restaurant on **Sass Pordoi** (2950m, 20min).

The 600m plunge to the road pass goes directly down that giddy gully L. ▶ Steps are followed down the initial steep part to easy zigzags, where scree running is feasible. The dangling cable-car is a constant overhead, while the magnificent Marmolada and its glacier are straight ahead.

> There may be snow at the top, even ice, so take extra care early in the season.

Amazing views from Sass Pordoi

At a grassy terrace populated by marmots and purple monkshood flowers, the path curves around a rock outcrop and large boulders, then widens and winds easily down across grass and dark earth to

1hr – Passo Pordoi (2239m). Hotel-grade accommodation only, such as Hotel Savoia ☎ 0462 601717, www.passo-pordoi.com. The lovely original décor, dating back to 1896, makes up for the unfriendly staff. SAD buses negotiate the hairpin bends E to Val Badia and W to Val di Fassa.

A 30min stroll SE along a narrow road is the stark Ossario, a military memorial and mausoleum with the remains of over 8000 German and Austrian troops who lost their lives in the Dolomites during the two world wars.

Between Casa Alpina and Hotel Savoia path n601/AV2 begins a gentle ascent around Sass Beccè past a chapel and romping marmots. Beyond rich gold carpets of globe flowers are beautiful views W to the majestic Catinaccio (amongst others) and very soon SE to the

STAGE 5 – RIFUGIO PISCIADÙ TO RIFUGIO CASTIGLIONI

Marmolada cradling its sprawling snowfield. A little further on the way curves L past **Rifugio Fredarola** (2400m) (☎ 0462 602072, sleeps 32, open 20 June to 20 Sept).

Now the Viel del Pan – a well-worn track wide enough for the mini tractor used by the hut ahead for transporting supplies – begins in earnest. It cuts E over slopes thick with an amazing wealth of wild blooms; black vanilla orchids and pasque flowers to mention but two. ▶ Not far along is a splendid natural podium for 'me and the Marmolada' snapshots.

Above are dark eroded volcanic cusps reminiscent of Easter Island statues.

Imagine a very thick slice of melon laid upon its side, and you will have a good bird's-eye notion of ... the Marmolata... or else you might think of a vast dead tooth stopped up with snow.

Reginald Farrer's delightful 1913 description.

1hr – Rifugio Viel del Pan (2432m) ☎ 0462 601720 or 0462 601323 sleeps 24, open 20 June to 20 Sept, www.rifugiovieldalpan.com. Cafeteria-style dining, no dorm but lovely rooms. Stunning position but nothing comes cheap here but the crowds in summer attest to the quality of the cooking.

The Marmolada from the Viel del Pan

TREKKING IN THE DOLOMITES

Approaching Lago di Fedaia

Reportedly the haunt of an ageing prince Vögle delle Velme when in a dark mood.

A bit quieter now, the path continues amidst wildflowers below castle-like Sasso Cappello (or Sas Ciapel) and the black lavic pinnacles Le Forfesc. ◄ A fork L to Porta Vescovo (cable-car link with Arabba) is ignored, and the descent S starts. Slippery if wet, it zigzags past a conifer or two and timber steps lead L around a rock face with several stretches of cable but minimal exposure. It quickly drops to the lakeside and

1hr 20min – Rifugio Castiglioni (2050m) ☎ 0462 601117 or 0462 601681, sleeps 50 in dorm and rooms, open spring to autumn, accepts credit cards. Wonderful establishment with cosy sleeping quarters, helpful staff and a dining room that gazes at the Marmolada.

On the roadside is a cluster of eateries and a bus stop for Dolomiti Bus runs E for Malga Ciapela (as well as Trentino Trasporti W to Val di Fassa).
The dam of Lago di Fedaia was constructed in 1956; it is 55m high, 342m long and holds 17 million cu.m of water, and serves the hydroelectric power station at Malga Ciapela.

STAGE 6
Rifugio Castiglioni to Passo San Pellegrino

Time	7hr
Distance	21.5km/13.4 miles
Ascent/Descent	1110m/1240m
Grade	2

Awfully long day but with plenty of variants in store. After the not especially exciting descent to Malga Ciapela (coverable by bus if desired), a rewarding traverse awaits. It entails at least 1000m uphill on a 1915–1918 military track for mules and men along with great views of the imposing 'back' side of the Marmolada and a host of outstanding Dolomites. A beautiful pasture valley lined with old photogenic hay barns leads to Passo San Pellegrino, where the stage staggers to a comfortable end.

However, the best advice is to make this a semi-rest day; stop at Malga Ciapela and treat yourself to an exhilarating ride on the three-stage cable-car to discover the breathtaking glaciated Marmolada. From the second station at 2950m explore Punta Serauta perforated with wartime tunnels, and visit the poignant WW1 museum; then travel by cable-car to the uppermost point, 3265m Punta Rocca, for spectacular 360° photo opportunities.

From **Rifugio Castiglioni** (2050m) cross the dam wall to restaurants and the lift to Pian dei Fiacconi and turn L (SE) along the old road, traffic free and peaceful above Lago di Fedaia, the name a reference to erstwhile grazing. A second dam wall and small lake are passed on the way to a bus stop and **Passo Fedaia** (2057m) and Rifugio Passo Fedaia ☎ 0437 722007 sleeps 25 (dorm and rooms), open late May to mid-Oct, credit cards.

On the R side of the road plunge down Pian di Lobia on a grassed ski slope (ESE) following the faint path. This

The climber's variant across the Marmolada is not described here, as ice equipment and experience is essential. For info and guides contact Rifugio Castiglioni.

Trekking in the Dolomites

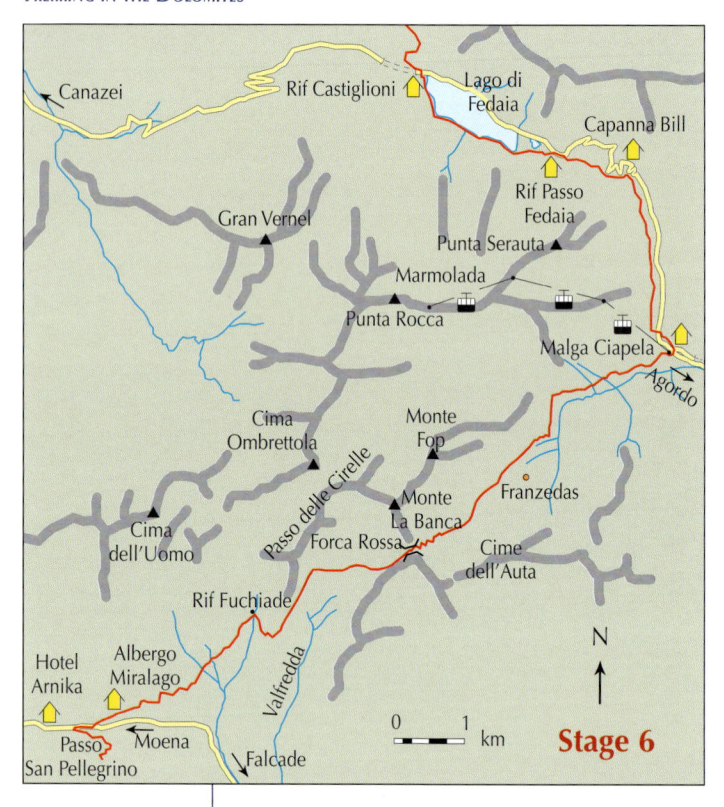

curves under a chair lift and crosses a stream continuing to 1780m roadside guesthouse **Capanna Bill** ☎ 0437 722100, open June to late Sept, www.capannabill.com.

Parallel to the road continue S down to the end of the chair lift for a series of tracks and past a ski lift through beautiful wood to Hotel Roy. ◀ It's not far down the road past the Marmolada cable-car (www.funiviemarmolada.com) to reach the handful of hotels that make up the resort of

> Views down the valley include the soaring points of the Cime dell'Auta S.

1hr 45min – Malga Ciapela (1384m). ATM, cafés and restaurants. Do any grocery shopping here, as there

Stage 6 – Rifugio Castiglioni to Passo San Pellegrino

THE MARMOLADA

The 'Queen of the Dolomites' stands 3342m high and 5km long. The earliest known summit attempt was in 1804 when a priest, doctor and lawyer set out to examine the glimmering ice sheet and put an end to superstitious beliefs. However, it was not until 1864 that Punta Penia, the highest elevation, was conquered by Grohmann and the Dimai brothers, his guides.

The age of the (rapidly shrinking) glacier is unknown. However, according to legend it was once lush and verdant pasture. One summer evening a lone old peasant stayed back to rake in her hay, as the weather appeared to be turning bad. Heedless of the admonitions from her companions, who were making for the valley to pay homage to the Virgin and invoke protection for the coming year, she pressed on with her labour. In next to no time she was caught up in a dramatic snow storm – sent as divine punishment! Alas, the weight of the deadly white cloak spelt her end, while the pastures hardened into the icy mass glacier that sprawls over the slope today.

She has not been alone in her icy tomb. The demarcation line between Italy and the former Hapsburg Empire ran the length of the crest and First World War soldiers perished on the treacherous high altitude terrain of the Marmolada – the Austrians lost 300 men alone in a single avalanche in December 1916. To shelter troops, the ingenious 'City of Ice', an astounding 12km network of tunnels was excavated deep in the glacier's eerie recesses. Survivors told of the uncanny pale blue light, then the spine-chilling creaks and groans of the ice grinding over rock.

---

are no further chances until the end of the trek without detouring off-route. Good value Hotel Tyrolia ☎ 0437 522999, credit cards, www.tyroliahotel.com. The nearest useful Tourist Office is at Rocca Pietore ⓘ 0437 721319, 5km away.

A matter of minutes downhill at Albergo Malga Ciapela turn R on the narrow road that follows Torrente Pettorina WSW through a camping ground. With short cuts it gains height in conifer wood thick with columbines and orchids and cows grazing in pasture clearings. The dramatic N wall of the Marmolada rears R, while ahead is triangular Monte Fop separating the Ombretta

TREKKING IN THE DOLOMITES

The uppermost cable-car on the Marmolada

and Franzedaz valleys. Past a summer dairy/restaurant is a bridge (1540m) – stick to the rough jeep track (n.689), soon veering due S. Ignore turn-offs for Rifugio Falier and wind SW in steady ascent through wood.

As the track turns dog-leg L to the scatter of summer farms that is Franzedas (1980), AV2 forks R on a signed path, whose WW1 military origin is soon evident for its gentle gradient and stone edging. The undergrowth is mostly larch, alpenrose and bilberry shrubs, while overhead is the magnificent spectacle of Monte Fop and Monte La Banca. The red earth fault where AV2 is heading is clearly in view now, albeit still a fair way off on the zigzags of the former mule track. Keep plodding on amidst bursts of bright wildflowers on the pale limestone and the darker earth. Purple milk vetch and delicate pink dwarf alpenrose stand out.

At last, on the low edge of Pizzo Le Crene, and easily recognisable for the black cloud of chattering alpine choughs hanging over it, is

3hr 15min – Forca Rossa (2490m), of strategic importance in WW1 for supplying the front that cut across the

STAGE 6 – RIFUGIO CASTIGLIONI TO PASSO SAN PELLEGRINO

Marmolada. Malga Ciapela can be seen in the valley, more than 1000m below! Once you've got your breath back you may be interested in the vast panorama ahead beyond the Cime dell'Auta, namely the San Martino altopiano and the jagged Focobon peaks – to be encountered first hand in the following stage.

Drop down the clear path SW (and ignore the fork R) across red clay terrain and grass. The path veers R (W) across two distinct pasture basins enjoyed by horses and marmots that attract birds of prey. A beautiful amphitheatre opens above backed by the Formenton-Sasso Valfredda barrier. Pian della Schita has lovely views down to the old dark timber huts lining Valfredda S. After a grassy ridge AV2 curves NW for the short drop to the immaculately kept meadows at the foot of the vast scree basin below Passo delle Cirelle ('gravel'), and popular family destination **Rifugio Fuchiade** (1982m), an upmarket restaurant, beautifully placed.

Now a traffic-free lane (n.607) makes its leisurely way SW past a string of photogenic hay barns and

It's a lovely stroll down to Passo San Pellegrino

125

TREKKING IN THE DOLOMITES

chalets and into light wood, eventually reaching Albergo Miralago ☎ 0462 573088, open year round exc. May and Nov, rooms and dorm accommodation, credit cards, good food, www.albergomiralago.com.

The hotel is 5min away from the road pass itself and the historic, if sadly ramshackle, pilgrims' hospice that gave the place its name.

2hr – Passo San Pellegrino (1919m), ATM, Trentino Trasporti buses to Moena in Val di Fassa (ⓘ 0462 609770) thence Trento, otherwise a rare Dolomiti Bus runs to Falcade (ⓘ 0437 599241).

More hotels are to be found on the western side of the pass such as Hotel Arnika ☎ 0462 573337, www.hotelarnika.it.

STAGE 7
Passo San Pellegrino to Rifugio Mulaz

Time	5hr 15min
Distance	13km/8 miles
Ascent/Descent	1346m/708m
Grade	3

This is quite a full-on stage, which passes through a brilliant range of scenery. It begins with a straightforward (Grade 2), if not exceptionally thrilling, traverse to Passo Valles, which hosts one of the best value refuge-cum-guesthouses on the AV2, a perfect place for taking a well-deserved break. Moreover, if desired, this opening section can be shortened by 1hr by taking the cable-car from Passo San Pellegrino to Col Margherita. **Note** In low cloud or mist with reduced visibility orientation and route-finding on this section could be difficult as waymarks are few and far between and landmarks rare.

STAGE 7 – PASSO SAN PELLEGRINO TO RIFUGIO MULAZ

> Once through Passo Valles a spectacular section emerges, as the trek enters the realms of the awesome Pale di San Martino, one of the most rugged Dolomite ranges. It boasts soaring elegant *campanile* towers around a vast altopiano, an authentic lunar upland. The highest summit is 3192m Cima Vezzena. All is well protected under the auspices of a Parco Naturale. The ensuing three stages are spent within its borders on an exciting roller coaster of sights and paths. However, this is not suitable terrain for beginners and in fact the stretch as far as Rifugio Mulaz, with exposed and aided passages, verges on quite difficult. An excellent easier alternative is to stick with the AV2 as far as either Forcella Venegia or Passo di Venegiota, then take the variant (a worthwhile route in itself). It rejoins the main trek 5hr on at Rifugio Rosetta at the end of Stage 8, but it can be shortened to 3hr by using public transport from Passo Rolle – see below.

From the main road at **Passo San Pellegrino** (1919m) turn across the main car park opposite the derelict refuge. Path n.658, signed for Passo Valles, strikes out SE across marshy terrain chopped up by hoofs of cows and horses that belong to the nearby farm. Planks have been laid across the worst bits. You quickly enter pretty wood and climb steadily, passing under the Col Margherita cable-car. Larch and juniper vegetation predominate and a cascading stream is crossed. As a ski piste is reached (45min) turn sharp R (W) uphill. Ahead is Col Margherita with its curious deep red porphyry column formations. The steep track rounds a corner and you keep L (SSE) for a further slog to

1hr – Corda degli Zingari (2297m), a broad crest on the edge of the Altipiano degli Zingari – a gently sloping upland scattered with boulders. The vast outlook takes in the Cima dell'Uomo and neighbours N, the magnificent Civetta E, and naturally the jagged towers of the Pale di San Martino ahead.

Leave the broad track (which continues to Col Margherita) and turn off L following cairns and red/white paint stripes over undulating terrain high above Lago di

Trekking in the Dolomites

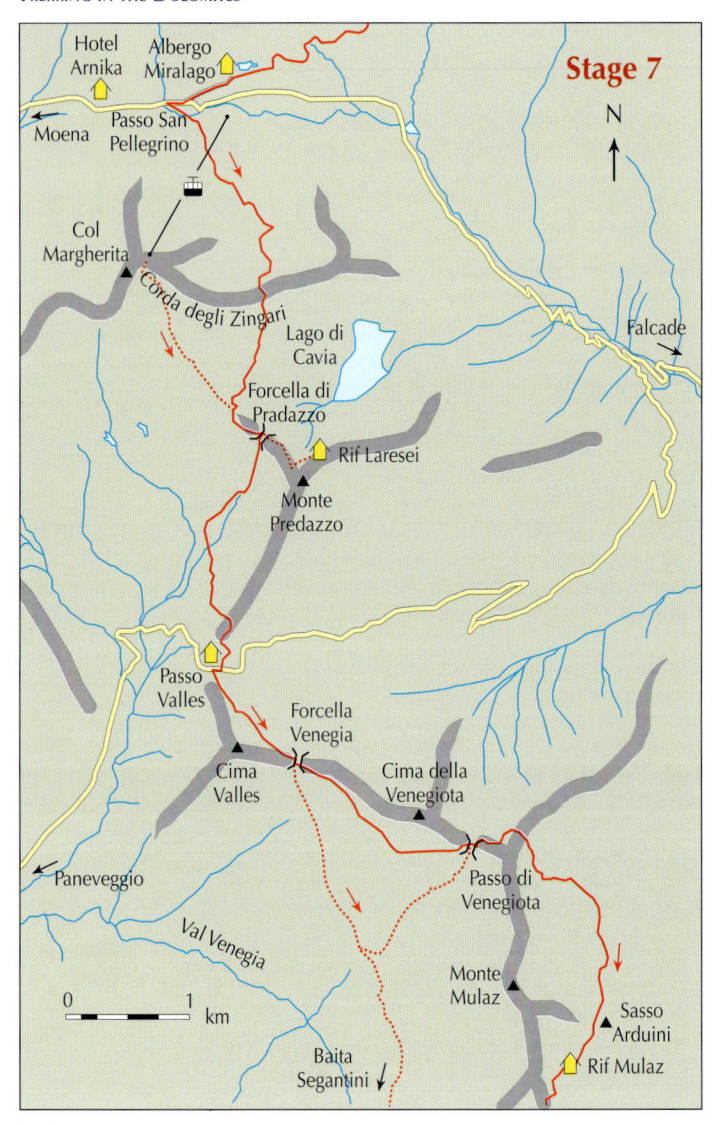

STAGE 7 – PASSO SAN PELLEGRINO TO RIFUGIO MULAZ

Cavia and its dam. Keep your eyes peeled for waymarks as it meanders amidst flowers and rock steps. A stretch S sees you join up briefly with a broad track (where the cable-car riders join up) – go L to the saddle and track intersection

30min – Forcella di Pradazzo (2220m).

> **Detour to Rifugio Laresei (30min)**
> For a good meal with a view or an overnight stay, you could do much worse than this bustling eatery-cum-refuge set on bald Monte Predazzo. Take the jeep track SE in gentle ascent from Forcella di Pradazzo. **Rifugio Laresei (2260m)** ☎ 0437 599000, sleeps 16, open June to Sept. It's worth the walk to taste their *torta di grano saraceno con frutti di bosco*, buckwheat cake with wild berries.

Head S down the dirt track beneath Monte Predazzo, cutting corners. Accompanied by clanging cow bells you have time to admire the spread of the vast slabs of the metamorphic Lagorai chain extending E-N. Past Malga Predazzo (2242m) it's not far to

30min – Passo Valles (2031m), with its excellent value family-run Rifugio Passo Valles ☎ 0437 599136, sleeps 40, open all year excluding Nov, credit cards www.passovalles.com. Of the superb meals to be enjoyed here, don't miss *Gnocchi di patate con ricotta affumicata* (delicate potato dumplings with smoked cheese). The ageing St Bernard dog is still in residence!

> To bail out here, walk down the road W. Only 3km away at the entrance to Val Venegia is Pian dei Casoni and a shuttle bus to Paneveggio and the Park Visitor Centre. Here are Trentino Trasporti buses to Predazzo in Val di Fassa, thence Trento, as well as via Passo Rolle to Fiera di Primiero and Feltre.

Across the road near the chapel, path n.751 climbs S zigzagging to the R of a sharp ridge, traversing impressive

Rifugio Passo Valles

grey-cream striations. Bearing SE over dark terrain well grassed and flowered, it ascends easily below Cima Valles to a crest and the notch of

30min – Forcella Venegia (2217m). Belonging to a magnificent line-up, Cimon della Pala (SSW), dubbed the 'Matterhorn of the Dolomites' for its slender form (but it is not the group's highest peak), lords it over deep Val Venegia; beyond stretches the Lagorai chain. Route variants depart from here.

Variants to Rifugio Rosetta
In order to bypass the following sections, which entail a series of steep and exposed tracts as far as Rifugio Rosetta, or in case of bad weather, a recommended option is to bail out at this point via path 749, which turns down R for pastoral Val Venegia, named by the Venetians who once exploited it for timber. There you join a rough road leading S and climbing to the restaurant **Baita Segantini** (2170m) – magnificently placed facing Cima della Vezzana, Cimon della Pala and the diminutive Travignolo hanging glacier.

STAGE 7 – PASSO SAN PELLEGRINO TO RIFUGIO MULAZ

> From here it is feasible to descend on foot, chairlift or summer bus past Capanna Cervino (☎ 0439 769095, www.capannacervino.it) to **Passo Rolle** (1980m, 2hr) for a coach to San Martino di Castrozza, thence a return to the main route on the plateau via the Col Verde gondola car then cable-car to Rifugio Rosetta. However, to cover the entire distance on foot, not far after the Baita Segantini chair lift, fork L on the faint unnumbered path that cuts S across marshy terrain and down past avalanche barriers to the road and **Malga Fosse di Sopra** summer dairy farm (1936m).
>
> Path n.712, 'Sentiero dei Finanzieri' (for the customs officers who created it) breaks off essentially SE. It gains ground over eroded gullies and terrain that features both muddy patches and fossilised ripple marks en route to **Crode Rosse** (2194m), a brilliant picnic spot.
>
> Continue ESE past marmot colonies and unless you opt for turn-off on n.706 leading to the cable-car at 1965m Col Verde (not such a bad idea in view of the near-vertical 500m climb that awaits!), stay high to slot into n.701. Zigzagging crazily as the modern cabins glide overhead, the exhilarating path climbs decidedly with occasional stretches of cable and minimal exposure. You stagger out at **Passo Rosetta** (2572m), a mere stroll from **Rifugio Rosetta** (2581m, 3hr) and the main route.
>
> **Timing** Allow 2hr for the Passo Rolle option and a further 1hr for buses and lifts. Otherwise it's 3hr 30min as far as Col Verde, and at least 5hr to Rifugio Rosetta on foot.

The path proceeds ESE along the grassy crest past a tiny lake and grazing sheep, dipping briefly SE to avoid Cima della Venegiota. With good chances of spotting marmots, it's not far to

45min – Passo di Venegiota (2302m). Here too it is possible to opt out and head for Passo Rolle (2hr), linking into path n.749 on the variant given above.

Now on the N side of Monte Mulaz the path passes across crumbly terrain accompanied by the first of a series of short but reassuring cables. A grassy shoulder opens on to a lengthy scree descent SE above a rock-strewn basin, while ahead the elegant Focobon peaks come into view a little at a time. A short, sheer cliff is rounded thanks to an

Climbing below Sasso Arduini, with a view to Falcade

aided section as AV2 moves S into upper Val di Focobon. Climbing steadily, it forks L up a rusty red gully equipped with long stretches of cable. Watch out for falling stones here. You emerge for a brief respite on a grassy flat but soon resume S following paint splashes and cables up pale rock slabs. A near-vertical section concludes at a col amidst myriad wildflowers for the short detour to 2582m Sasso Arduini, a wonderful belvedere named after a president of the Venice branch of the Italian Alpine Club who constructed the refuge, only a stone's throw away. This is also a magnificent viewpoint for the fantastic Focobon peaks and remnant hanging glacier with recognisable moraine ridges. The name may derive from *buon fuoco*, or 'fire', referring to the reddish reflected sun's rays caught by the peaks.

A brief path downhill leads to spectacularly positioned

2hr – Rifugio Mulaz (2571m), ☎ 0437 599420, CAI, sleeps 52, open 20 June to 20 Sept. Water is deemed unsuitable for drinking. The delicious *pasta con ragù* comes in mountainous servings. State-of-the-art technology powers the building and the hot shower, which is pricey but powerful.

The elegant Civetta is visible NE. The hut's full name is Rifugio Giuseppe Volpi al Mulaz, in memory of the Venetian entrepreneur count who launched the city's mainland industrial development in the 1910s, along with the now world-famous film festival. Mulaz on the other hand is probably related to 'mule' for the shape of the adjacent mountain.

For those with energy to burn, from the refuge's rocky platform a well-marked and straightforward path climbs NNW to the panoramic summit of 2906m **Monte Mulaz** in 45min.

Exit is feasible by way of path n.710 via nearby Passo del Mulaz to upper Val Venegia thence Baita Segantini (2hr 10min) – see variant above.

STAGE 8
Rifugio Mulaz to Rifugio Rosetta

Time	4hr 15min
Distance	8km/5 miles
Ascent/Descent	860m/850m
Grade	3+

Massively rewarding and extremely tiring stage that takes AV2 walkers across rugged passages into the breathtaking heart of the Pale di San Martino where humans are but minuscule dots on an immense limestone rockscape that extends for over 50km^2. A good head for heights, no vertigo, and a sure foot are essential, along with good stable weather. Early summer walkers may need an ice axe to deal with hard snow – enquire of the Rifugio Mulaz guardian if in doubt before setting out. ▶

TREKKING IN THE DOLOMITES

> First off is a short traverse and dizzy aided climb to Passo delle Farangole on a well maintained path. A vertical gully is then negotiated with the help of cable. The delicate scent in the air comes from the pretty yellow poppies that miraculously bloom in these apparently desolate surrounds. The path heads downhill through chamois country for a marvellous, lengthy traverse with stunning views, the 'Sentiero delle Farangole' high over Val delle Comelle, dwelling place of nymphs capable of whisking away a man's reason. Once Pian dei Cantoni is reached, all that remains is a steady ascent onto the limestone plateau and lunar landscape of San Martino to a comfortable rifugio. Take care on this final stretch as orientation can be a problem in the mist, which can roll in at the drop of a hat even on a bright sunny day, obscuring useful landmarks.

Leave **Rifugio Mulaz** (2571m) uphill on n.703, which soon forks L to zigzag up a path reinforced with tree trunks to the notch of **Forcella Margherita** (2655m). Now beneath soaring Cima del Focobon it traverses a vast scree basin where snow lingers, before heading E, ever steeper, towards that deep cut between two *campanile*

Passo delle Farangole squeezed between rock towers

STAGE 8 – RIFUGIO MULAZ TO RIFUGIO ROSETTA

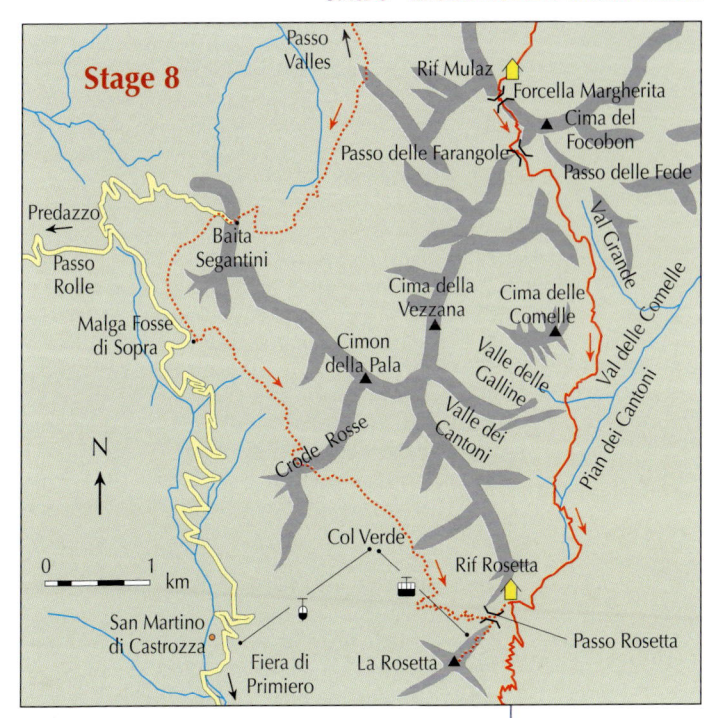

towers. Steel staples and lengths of cable help you scramble up to

1hr 15min – Passo delle Farangole (2814m), a dizzy perch, the apt name means 'deep incision'.

Take special care on the next section not to dislodge stones, which could endanger other walkers. The ensuing plunge sticks close to the L side with lengths of cable all the way down this vertical chimney, concluding with rungs and a ladder. At the bottom keep L on easier, if mobile, scree, where fleet-hoofed chamois may be seen. Down into the basin of broken rock curve R past 2675m Passo delle Fede, a reference to the sheep that once grazed up here.

Bearing S over Val Grande you drop steadily over grass-flower terrain at the foot of soaring peaks. The undulating lunar Altipiano di San Martino spreads out SE. Soon, hundreds of metres below is the dramatic trough of sheer-sided Val delle Comelle. Valstrut opens up W from a 2290m fork for Bivacco Brunner and 3192m Cima della Vezzana, the highest in this group and destination for mountaineers.

Proceeding S the path feels a little exposed and vertiginous as it cuts across sheer rugged mountainsides. After a grassy shoulder studded with edelweiss and alpine thrift, it begins to climb once more, overshadowed by Cima delle Comelle. Long aided stretches cross rock faces before a shallow chasm and a narrow chimney at the foot of Valle delle Galline ('chickens'). At last a broad pasture corner dotted with boulders is gained and there are satisfying views back over the path covered.

A gentle gradient dips into a vast atmospheric basin with blinding white rivers of scree carpeted with fragrant yellow poppies.

2hr 15min – Pian dei Cantoni (2313m) is surrounded by spectacular peaks. Joined by a path from Gares at the northern base of Val delle Comelle, n.703 begins the day's final climb. Marked by the odd red/white paint splash and cairns, it makes its way up to the vast undulating plateau pitted with a surprising number of limestone dolina depressions, filled either with snow or tiny baby gentians which survive on a thin layer of accumulated soil detritus blown in by the wind. Rearing ESE is the Pala di San Martino mountain, recognisable for its vertical grooves. At a signed junction AV2 joins an old military track in remarkably good condition, and at the very last minute sees and gains

45min – Rifugio Rosetta (2581m) aka Rifugio Giovanni Pedrotti ☎ 0439 68308, CAI, sleeps 80, open 20 June to 20 Sept, credit cards, www.rifugiorosetta.it. The water is not drinkable. Generous servings of dishes such as flavoursome *Canederli* (dumplings) are served in the bustling dining room.

STAGE 8 – RIFUGIO MULAZ TO RIFUGIO ROSETTA

The spacious refuge dates back to 1890. However, it was burnt down in both world wars, to be rebuilt and since enlarged by SAT, the Trento branch of the Italian Alpine Club, who named it after their past president. Luckily, recent renovation has not robbed it of its old alpine-style charm in the dorms and timber hallways.

Do find the time for a side trip to La Rosetta.

Rifugio Rosetta

Side trip to La Rosetta (1hr return)
On a clear day the easy 2743m summit of La Rosetta is highly recommended. 'Rosetta' or 'rosy' is the delicate pinkish hue the mountain assumes with the first rays of morning sun. Follow the path SW towards the cable-car, then turn off up the vast incline to the 'pulpit' and cross at the top for heart-stopping views down over the township of San Martino di Castrozza and beyond to the metamorphic Lagorai chain, a veritable plethora of Dolomites, and even the glaciated Ortles-Cevedale groups in the distant WNW. What's more this viewpoint helps to understand the Altipiano di San Martino, the seemingly endless barren upland smoothed by bodies of ice 10,000 years ago and subsequently further eroded into karst. Outstanding are neighbours Croda della Pala N and Cimon della Pala NNW, but record-holder Vezzana N is partially concealed. The view SSE takes in Passo del Ball, crossed tomorrow.

If you must, this is a good place to join or leave the AV2 thanks to the nearby cable-car to Col Verde thence the lift and shuttle bus to the chic alpine resort of San Martino di Castrozza. Otherwise on foot via exhilarating path n.701 – allow 1hr 30min to Col Verde, and the same again to San Martino ⓘ 0439 768867. Hotels, hostel ☎ 0439 769166, www.ostellodolomiti.com, groceries, ATM, frequent Trentino Trasporti coaches run via Fiera di Primiero to Feltre and trains.

STAGE 9
Rifugio Rosetta to Rifugio Treviso

Time	6hr 15min
Distance	14km/8.7 miles
Ascent/Descent	820m/1770m
Grade	3

A curious story is behind the former mule track followed on the opening stretch. Leaving the outskirts of San Martino to climb up Val di Roda to the actual plateau, a total ascent of 1000m (tunnel included), it was the brain-child of Leipzig native Baron von Lesser. He funded it with lotteries and personal donations from 1905 to 1912, when the area belonged to the Hapsburg Empire. As the story goes, workers were paid by the metre rather than on a time basis and ingeniously stretched out the path, judging from its interminable zigzags (240 in all) and all but imperceptible height gain! In another version the gentle gradient was intentional so as to ensure a smooth ride on horseback for his disabled daughter, so she could admire the wonders on high.

A magnificent traverse ensues to excellent Rifugio Pradidali, a good place to overnight. However, be aware that after the mule track it includes a long aided stretch, which is exciting but pretty exposed, not everyone's cup of tea; to be avoided at all costs in wet weather, when it can be dangerous.

STAGE 9 – RIFUGIO ROSETTA TO RIFUGIO TREVISO

After the refuge comes another difficult, but shorter, passage leading up Passo delle Lede, then a never-ending winding descent that touches on a beautifully placed unmanned bivouac hut. It all comes to a happy conclusion at a refuge in the welcoming cover of wood in beautiful Val Canali, another of the wonders of the Pale di San Martino. However, all this is easily avoided thanks to a lovely lower path that loops through Val Canali – see below.

Lastly, those short of time may like to embark on the short cut to Passo delle Lede – see below.

From **Rifugio Rosetta** (2581m) turn R (S) on broad stony track n.702 via Passo di Val Roda (2572m) for the drop to skirt the base of Croda di Roda. The bleached mountainsides contrast strongly with the dark, almost luscious, green of the forested valleys far below, while the rock faces close at hand harbour a host of flowers such as saxifrages, thrift and the divine Moretti's bellflower – an endemic. Eventually, 300m lower, you veer L (E) along manmade ledges rounding **Col delle Fede** (2278m), a grassed outcrop studded with edelweiss and once of importance for grazing, judging by its name. A level stretch leads E across a scree valley flanking impressive Pala di San Martino, and a glimpse of a surviving pocket glacier. Not far on, where the old mule track continues its crazy zigzagging descent W for San Martino, AV2/n.715 breaks off SSE keeping to the L flank of a desolate snow-streaked valley to avoid its rubble-filled centre. Soon, following a warning sign suggesting inexperienced walkers rope up and use karabiners, is the beginning of guiding cable anchored to the rock as you edge along narrow ledges and clamber hands-on up rock faces, to be tackled with the appropriate care. The going can be pretty giddy and extremely beautiful. A path reappears for the final clamber to

2hr – Passo del Ball (2443m), named in honour of John Ball, one of the initiators of Dolomite mountaineering and first president of the Alpine Club. A dramatic

After the rigours of yesterday's Farangole crossing you may like to make this a semi-rest day and split the stage into more manageable sections, giving yourself more time to fully enjoy the breathtaking landscapes.

TREKKING IN THE DOLOMITES

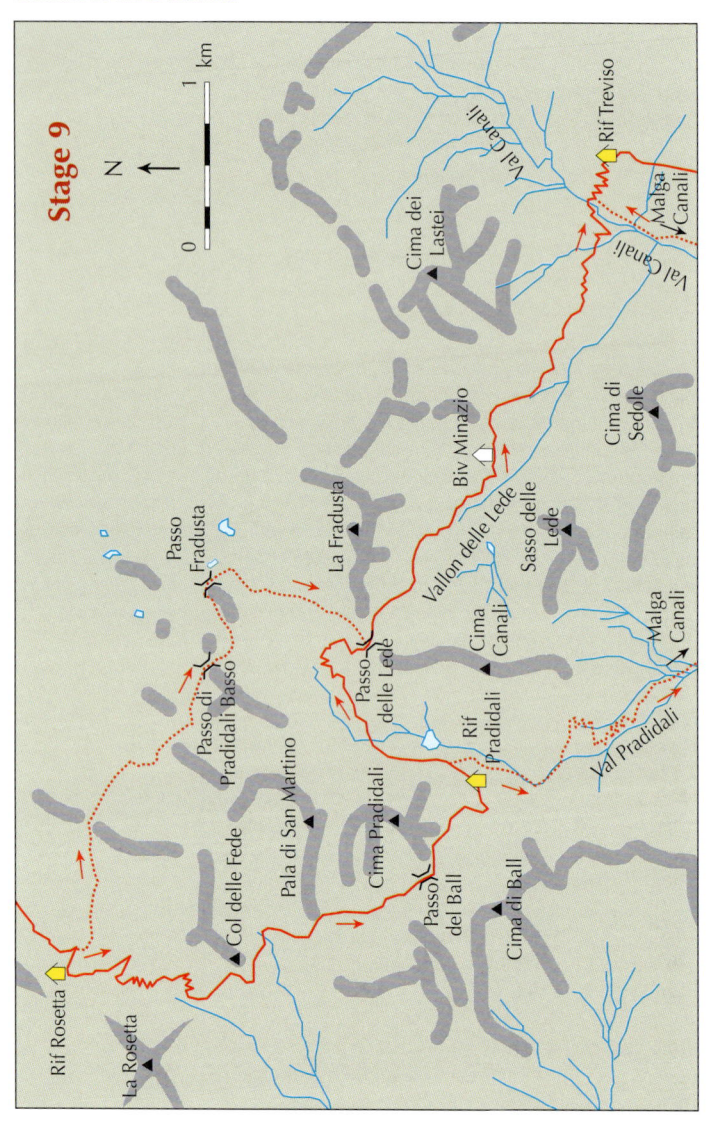

opening between Cima di Ball SW and Cima Pradidali NE, it grants your first view of awesome Cima Canali E, while S impressive Sass Maor stands out, with the Vette Feltrine beyond.

N.715 continues in an easy descent E, dodging toppled boulders and scree to

25min – Rifugio Pradidali (2278m), CAI, ☎ 0439 64180, sleeps 64, open mid-June to end Sept, www.rifugiopradidali.com.

A brand new establishment to replace the sorely missed historic timber-panelled building erected back in 1896 by the Dresden Alpine Club, and which once hosted the King of Belgium. Run by a knowledgeable alpine guide, it is still a welcoming place and has a dining room with huge glass windows; the water is undrinkable. The name may derive from the *prati gialli* (yellow meadows) down in the valley, possibly for the profuse poppies. However, the refuge's first name was Pravitali Hütte.

For walkers who prefer to avoid the steep crossing of Passo delle Lede, a variant is given.

Easy variant to Rifugio Treviso (3hr 15min)
From Rifugio Pradidali (2278m) descend S on path n.709, zigzagging down the head of Val Pradidali, on steep stretches aided by guiding cables. Brilliant alpine flowers can be observed here. Lower down are pine forest and easier gradients. Some 1hr 30min in descent turn L as per signposting for Malga Canali and Rifugio Treviso (unless you prefer to drop a further 30min to 1180m and Cant del Gal guesthouse ☎ 0439 62997, sleeps 24, open year-round, restaurant, parking, bus to Fiera di Primiero ⓘ 0439 62407, shops and hotels such as B&B Villa Sole ☎ 0439 62337, www.villasole.tn.it). A delightful undulating path through shady wood leads around NE for Malga Canali (1302m) (meals) in a lovely setting. After a parking area, track n.707 leads N up Val Canali to cross the watercourse R and start the climb E, joined by the main AV2 route for Rifugio Treviso.

Aided stretch to Passo del Ball

STAGE 9 – RIFUGIO ROSETTA TO RIFUGIO TREVISO

Once you can drag yourself away from the comforts of the refuge, head N up the immense valley on n.709 in the shadow of towering Cima Canali and Cima Wilma. A clear path across smashed rock leads around Lago Pradidali, silted up in late summer but has a pretty green hue earlier in the season. After an outcrop it bears R, gaining considerable height via a series of terraces.

Some 40min up is a signed junction where n.711/AV2 forks R (NE). It shortly enters a chaotic rubble-choked gully, hugging the L flank – watch out for stones dislodged by walkers above. An alternative soon presents itself: either stick to the near-vertical gully or fork L onto the rock face for a scramble up the exposed rock face. The two join forces 50m up on a detritus terrace, the worst behind you now. So relax and take in the amazing views that range as far as the Marmolada NE.

Keep your eyes peeled for red paint marks E for the most part, several easy hands-on bits but no exposure. Only metres before the saddle, you're joined by a short cut from Rifugio Rosetta.

> **Short cut from Rifugio Rosetta to Passo delle Lede (1hr 30min)**
> **Note** This route is only feasible late in the season when the snow has melted and the route becomes visible. Check conditions before leaving the refuge.
> From Rifugio Rosetta (2581m) path n.708 climbs E across the plateau via Passo di Pradidali Basso and onto Passo Fradusta (2704m). Here red marks (without numbers) point SSW skirting the wild head of the valley well below the Fradusta and its shrinking ice field, to Passo delle Lede (2695m) and the main AV2.

1hr 30min – Passo delle Lede (2695m), a breathtaking spot! The Pala di San Martino and partner Cima Immink steal the show W, while La Fradusta does its best to impress E. The E side of the pass is quite different, desolate Vallon delle Lede is wilder and apparently only visited by walkers on the AV2. A good path drops SE across scree towards flowered patches and pasture enjoyed by sheep, overshadowed by Cima Wilma and Canali. It's not

Trekking in the Dolomites

Taking it easy at Rifugio Treviso

STAGE 9 – RIFUGIO ROSETTA TO RIFUGIO TREVISO

long until you pass scattered debris of a US plane that crashed here in 1956. Coming into sight at the very last minute is

50min – Bivacco Minazio (2295m). A sturdy wooden hut with bunk beds and blankets for 12, and water nearby. Intending users will need their own stove and utensils.

Rifugio Treviso (the day's destination) can be spotted ensconced in trees on the opposite side of Val Canali, not to mention the rugged crest with tomorrow's route.

In relentless descent surrounded by throngs of delightful edelweiss, the gradient steepens as the path snakes down the valley middle with short hands-on rock faces soon reaching the 2000m mark, where springy dwarf mountain pine and spruce appear. Further down you veer L across a bleached stream bed under Pala dei Colombi, loose stones underfoot and increased steepness making for tiring going. Shady beech wood is quite enjoyable after days on end of rockscapes, and bird song here is divine. Keeping L at a fork (R is an exit route to Cant del Gal and bus stop) a soft path leads to a bridge (1450m) over a gushing river, but a stream soon requires leaping over.

Now gird your loins as a wide path is joined for the last 25min leg in gentle ascent through wood and past waterfalls, to

1hr 30min – Rifugio Treviso (1631m), so named for the branch of the Alpine Club that owns it. ☎ 0439 62311, CAI, sleeps 44, open June 20 to end Sept, credit cards, www.rifugiotreviso.it. Hospitable place run by a knowledgeable alpine guide, it has undergone extensive modernisation throughout and now boasts lovely bathrooms, while retaining the comfortable dining room and old fireplace, as well as creaky timber floors and some old sleeping cubicles upstairs. Power comes from the turbine set at the nearby waterfall. This is a VIP base for climbers who easily outnumber AV2 walkers as it is said that Val Canali boasts the best limestone in the whole of the Dolomites.

TREKKING IN THE DOLOMITES

Many visitors come for the food: the minestrone is especially delicious while an unusual dish is *carne salada con fagioli*, thinly sliced cured beef seasoned with lemon and served with brown beans.

STAGE 10
Rifugio Treviso to Passo Cereda

Time	4hr 30min
Distance	9km/5.6 miles
Ascent/Descent	1100m/1370m
Grade	2–3

A very enjoyable stroll through cool forest opens this stage; next comes a steepish climb to a strategic col. Here AV2 bids farewell to the spectacular Pale di San Martino as vistas open onto the Cimònega and Vette Feltrine chains, where AV2 will spend its concluding days. In the meantime a couple of hours are spent on the equivalent of a partly exposed goat's path skirting crumbling gullies and steep slopes where overhangs are festooned with colourful blooms. A sure foot is essential here. The sound of 'civilisation' wafts up from farming communities far below: wood chopping, dogs barking, cows mooing. The day wraps up with a knee-testing descent to meadows and a rural road pass where comfortable refuge-hotels await. Here buses are on hand for walkers who decide to call it a day, so as to avoid the testing wild paths ahead on the final three stages.

On the other hand, should you not feel up to this strenuous crossing, by all means follow the route as far as the Campigol d'Oltro junction then fork R in descent to Val Canali thence Cant del Gal (2hr) – see the variant in Stage 9 for practical info.

Turn L out of the front door of **Rifugio Treviso** (1631m) along the side wall with its sundial. Heading S, path n.718 crosses the first of three boulder-choked gullies.

146

STAGE 10 – RIFUGIO TREVISO TO PASSO CEREDA

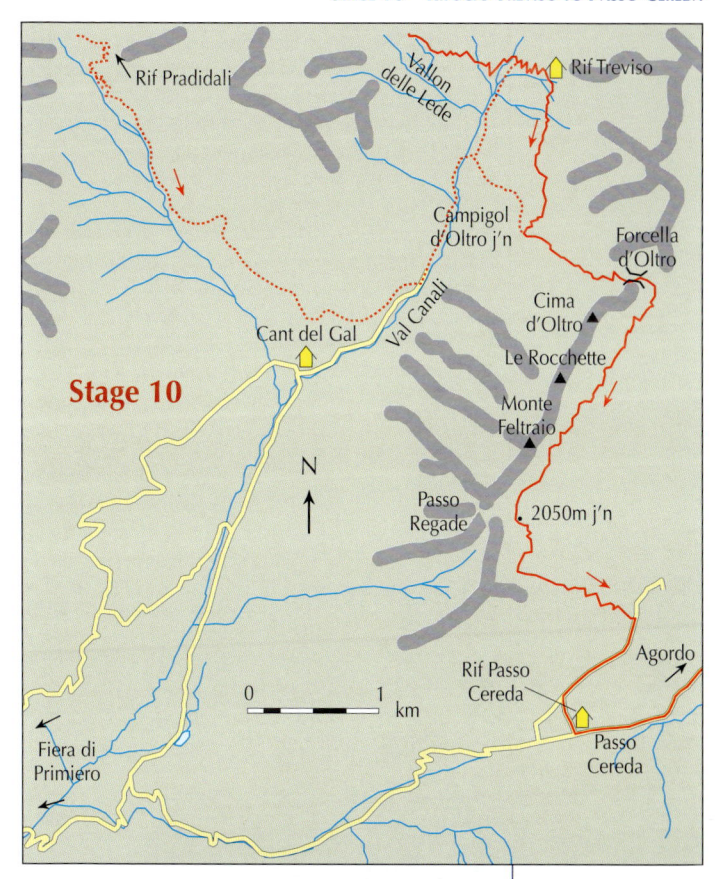

In beech and pine forest pretty with purple orchids and adenostyle, it continues mostly on a level. Views across Val Canali open up of Vallon delle Lede flanked on either side by soaring rock towers.

40min – Campigol d'Oltro junction (1730m). Here AV2 forks L (SE) to start the ascent, in the company of shy chamois. Thick shrub vegetation and dwarf mountain

TREKKING IN THE DOLOMITES

pines give way to larch and alpenrose cover, then stones and sparse grass on this relentless but straightforward ascent. Higher up, the path moves to the L of the valley to avoid snow tongues. Make the most of getting-your-breath-back pauses to admire elegant Sass Maor due W and upper Vallon delle Lede visited yesterday.

1hr – Forcella d'Oltro (2094m) and its pointed rock sentinel. This is the easternmost edge of the Pale di San Martino, and the pass affords a vast outlook over rolling woodland and meadows, quite a contrast to the last few days! From here on, expect to see spectacular clumps of the endemic bloom Moretti's bellflower sheltering in rock overhangs.

Watch your step, as the path immediately drops steeply on loose stones, bearing R to begin its long traverse SW. The going is pretty narrow and exposed in stretches, on grassy earth and rock terrain. It skirts sheer flanks below Cima d'Oltro then Le Rocchette. Passo Duran visited on AV1 can be seen NE flanked by the Moiazza and San Sebastiano chains, while below

The long traverse after Forcella d'Oltro

STAGE 10 – RIFUGIO TREVISO TO PASSO CEREDA

nestles the farming village of Gosaldo. Then SE is the spread of the rugged Cimònega group and the complete sequence of the Vette Feltrine, explored by the AV2 starting tomorrow.

After Monte Feltraio it climbs to the 2100m mark and finally reaches a strategic **2050m junction** (1hr 20min) below Passo Regade. Bizarre stone pinnacles stick out of the mountainsides here.

Brace your knees for the steep descent SE as the path weaves its way through what resembles a petrified forest interspersed with live conifers. It's pretty spectacular not to mention fatiguing.

An abrupt veer L (E) heads over loose stones and quickly into cooler woodland where the gradient eases and leaves and pine needles underfoot make for softer going. A good hour from the Regade junction, a narrow surfaced road is finally reached at 1450m. Turn R (SW) for a leisurely stroll past meadows with barns. As you approach the pass, leave the road at the first building for an unmarked path that brings you out alongside Rifugio Passo Cereda.

Descent path to Passo Cereda

TREKKING IN THE DOLOMITES

> Trentino Trasporti buses here to Fiera di Primiero and connections to Feltre for trains.

2hr 50min – Passo Cereda (1360m) belongs to a pastoral area, and faces the light grey rock points of Pale del Garofolo. Accommodation and memorable meals at **Rifugio Passo Cereda** ☎ 0439 65118-65030, sleeps 65, open all year exc. Nov, credit cards, www.passocereda.com or nearby Agritur Broch ☎ 0439 65028, www.agriturismobroch.it; both have dorms. ◄

STAGE 11
Passo Cereda to Rifugio Boz

Time	7hr 15min
Distance	14km/8.7 miles
Ascent/Descent	1060m/700m
Grade	3+

Today the trek makes its way across the Cimònega group to enter the Parco Naturale delle Dolomiti Bellunesi, a region of great wild natural beauty, brilliant endemic flora – and very few walkers. Rugged, wild and exciting days lie ahead. This long stage is breathtaking non-stop. However, demanding is the flavour of the day as things are not exactly straightforward. The ascent to Forcella Comedon is arguably the most challenging stretch on the whole of the AV2 and should not be under-rated or embarked upon in anything but good, stable weather. The terrain is unstable and the higher stretch subject to erosion, as it gets progressively eaten away by heavy rains. Next, upper Val Canzoi is traversed by way of a well-marked path through a magnificent amphitheatre where Bivacco Feltre-Bodo stands – do consider an overnight stay if you can rustle up some food and cooking equipment beforehand, as it will make the follow-on more enjoyable.

The ensuing section traverses a breathtaking valley on a narrow path cutting the flanks of Sass de Mura in a blaze of wildflowers. This long day comes to an end at hospitable 'log cabin' Rifugio Boz which excels at feeding starving AV2 walkers.

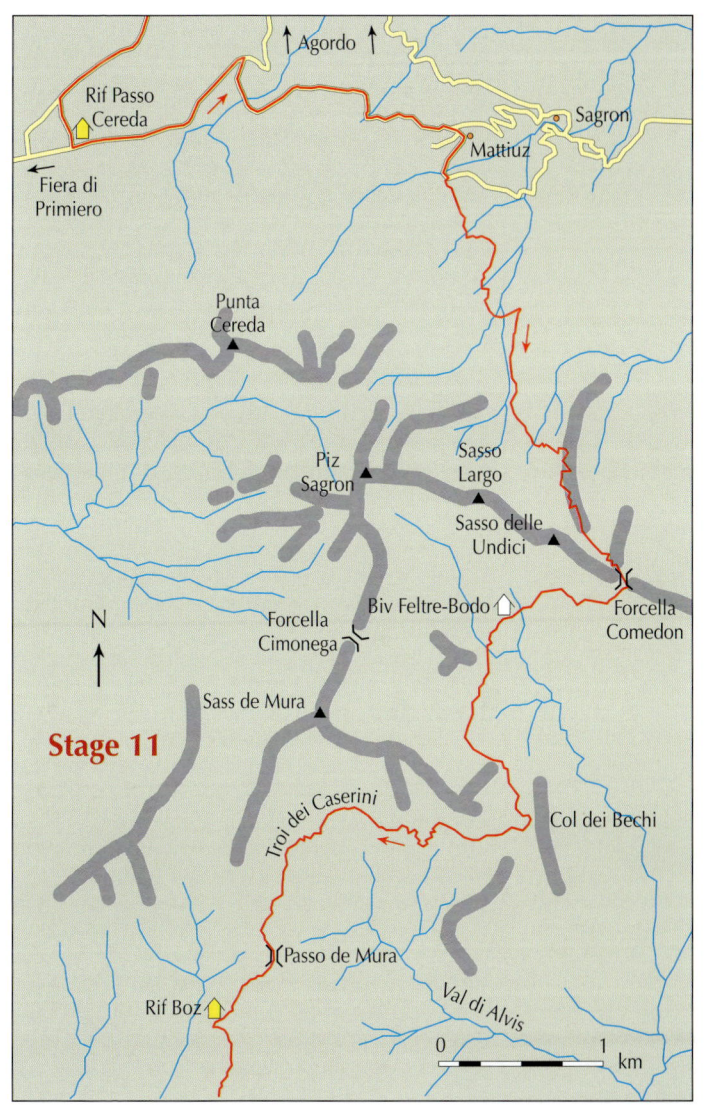

Stage 11 – Passo Cereda to Rifugio Boz

Turn L (ENE) at **Passo Cereda** (1360m) down the road looking over to the San Sebastiano group and past farms and pasture. A quarter of an hour along, take the minor road R through two camping grounds. Mostly E, this proceeds through pretty wood. The minute the trees are left behind fork R (n.801, sign for Sagron) to reach the hamlet of **Mattiuz** (1201m, 45min) with its fountain and handful of houses. Only minutes down the road S is a marked turn-off R for n.801. The way is not immediately clear so keep an eye out for red/white markings veering L across meadow and into conifer wood where a faint, and occasionally muddy, path leads across streams with moss-ridden rocks. It climbs gently to cross a dirt lane at the foot of **Piz Sagron**, becoming much clearer but a new stretch (differing from maps) soon detours across a stream – watch out for waymarks. This finally emerges from tree cover onto bleached broken rock and superb views over farming hamlets backed by Monte Agner N and Civetta NNE, to name just two. Scattered larch and dwarf mountain pine accompany to where the original path is joined beneath sheer rock walls. Mostly SSE n.801 heads across a messy rubble gully and zigzags to a saddle under Sasso Largo.

On this stretch quite a few lengths of cable attached to the cliffs are of help, while a sequence of oblique ledges make for pleasurable walking. At rest stops check the rock faces for the exquisite devil's claw blooms. Hugging the flanks of **Sasso delle Undici** little by little things deteriorate and, for the concluding 200m, you find yourself struggling up soft, moving scree where it can get a bit tricky, the near-vertical gradient adding difficulty. Progress can be painstaking as rain and erosion have produced a series of precarious crests that necessitate lots of hands-on clambering. It's quite a relief to stagger out at

4hr 15min – Forcella Comedon (2067m), an old smugglers' pass belonging to the Parco Nazionale delle Dolomiti Bellunesi. Once you've got your breath back, face S to appreciate the emerald green of Lago della Stua in Valle Canzoi at your feet.

STAGE 11 – PASSO CEREDA TO RIFUGIO BOZ

The path turns R (W) to a notch thence a broken-rock gully descent to the beautiful cirque where a carpet of edelweiss surrounds the two corrugated iron huts of

Clambering up to Forcella Comedon

30min – Bivacco Feltre-Bodo (1930m). Bunks and blankets for 15, water nearby.

Piz Sagron dominates NW, kept company by Sasso Largo and Sasso delle Undici.

N.801 heads S downhill past lovely waterfalls and a fork (where n.806 drops rapidly to Val Canzoi and 660m Albergo Boz ☎ 0439 43145, at the start of a 7km road to Soranzen thence year-round Dolomiti Bus service to Feltre). Making a semi-circle of this spectacular upper valley, the path zigzags steeply and relentlessly up to **Col dei Bechi** (1960m, 1hr) on a dizzy narrow

Trekking in the Dolomites

Waterfall on the way to Col dei Bechi

STAGE 11 – PASSO CEREDA TO RIFUGIO BOZ

ridge where chamois hang out. The rugged spine and peaks of the Vette Feltrine unfold ahead SW, an inspiring sight. The route here is known as the *Troi dei Caserini*, the 'way of the shepherds', who used it until recently. Narrow, but clear, it soon descends W to avoid an old landslip before returning uphill to hug the stark rock face which is studded with wonderful flowers, like endemic columbines. Trickling cascades are crossed under magnificent Sass de Mura, which simply takes your breath away. Curving S high over the head of Val di Alvis, the concluding tract to the pass entails a couple more tricky passages, including a short aided stretch. In the vicinity of wartime tunnels gouged out of the rock, the main grassy crest is gained then

2hr 15min – Passo de Mura (1867m), a broad saddle with great views. The modern-day boundary separating the regions of Trentino and Veneto, this once separated the Hapsburg Empire from the Kingdom of Italy, hence the vestiges of the military track, still recognisable.

Sharing a muddy path with the cows, you head SW over pasture to

15min – Rifugio Boz (1718m) ☎ 0439 64448, CAI, sleeps 36, open 20 June to 20 Sept and weekends May and Oct. Local dairy products are served, such as *schiz* – a fresh local cheese that is pan-fried with cream. The cosy dining room of this modest converted farm is warmed by a log fire.

The outlook is towards a curious bank of light grey rock with soaring bastions and striking parallel strata verging on the horizontal. These are the Vette Feltrine; traversed in their entirety tomorrow. Sweet dreams!

If necessary the village of Imer in Val Noana (Trentino Trasporti buses to Feltre) can be reached. Take path n.727, which joins a stony track SW via Rifugio Fonteghi (☎ 0439 67043 private, sleeps 18, www.rifugiofonteghi.com), thereafter surfaced road.

STAGE 12
Rifugio Boz to Rifugio Dal Piaz

Time	6hr
Distance	15km/9.3 miles
Ascent/Descent	870m/600m
Grade	3

Exhilarating, awesome and unforgettable conclusion (almost) to the AV2, this stage is a drawn-out traverse of the wildly beautiful Vette Feltrine. A world unto themselves, this string of rugged peaks and contiguous valleys is carefully safeguarded under the auspices of a special reserve within the national park for scientific reasons. Visitors are requested not to leave marked paths or gather any vegetable or mineral specimens. Interest levels are high for flora and geology buffs – the concluding section features fossil-rich *rosso ammonitico* rock with flint insets. Fish teeth, sea urchins and myriad shells have been found – Rifugio Dal Piaz has an interesting display.

In terms of difficulty, one section stands out: Passo di Finestra to Sassio di Scarnia is no Sunday stroll, but constantly exposed and necessitates a sure foot and no problems with vertigo. Thereafter the going is relatively more straightforward, with a better path on easier terrain. Further on is Piazza del Diavolo; the uncannily silent 'devil's square' used to be a favourite haunt of witches and other practitioners of evil. However, it is now safe to cross thanks to the priest from Vignui, a nearby village, who banished them by planting a huge cross there.

A final 'but' concerns the mist that can rise unexpectedly from the adjoining plain, quickly shrouding the mountains and obstructing views and landmarks. Otherwise the stage is extraordinarily scenic! It goes without saying that good weather conditions are essential as otherwise it could be, frankly, dangerous; escape routes are few and far between. Carry plenty of drinking water.

From **Rifugio Boz** (1718m) n.801/AV2 strikes out S negotiating an especially muddy livestock path across the light wooded flanks of Colsent.

Stage 12 – Rifugio Boz to Rifugio Dal Piaz

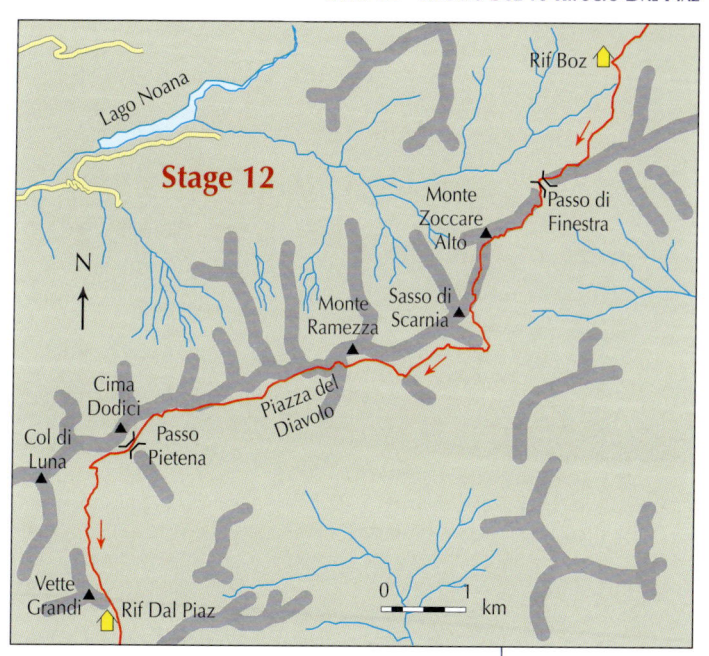

40min – Passo di Finestra (1766m), 'window pass', where in fact views open up towards the Veneto plain. If the weather doesn't look good, exit on n.805 in descent SE to a track leading to Albergo Boz in Val Canzoi (see Stage 11 for practical details).

Keep R (SW) now for a remarkable path, heritage of hunters and soldiers. Hewn into the rock face at times, a little narrow and exposed as it crosses eroded gullies, it proceeds SW below Monte Zoccare Alto through a veritable rock garden. Sprays of slender long-stemmed edelweiss alternate with milky saxifrage and dazzling blue Moretti's bellflower, very much at home here. ▶ A tricky passage fitted with a reassuring stretch of hand cable is followed by an exposed narrow neck. Steps then zigzag upwards through bushy vegetation to more cable and

> Watch your rucksack doesn't catch on the frequent overhangs.

157

Approaching Piazza del Diavolo

another dizzy neck bridge where a clear head and sure foot is essential. Then what feels like a near-vertical goat's path leads up a spur to

2hr – 2060m shoulder, at the base of soaring Sasso di Scarnia. The worst is behind you now as things improve a fair bit, but there's still a long way to go.

Through a maze of boulders, AV2 heads due S in descent with a few clambers but no exposure (the dots on the Tabacco map are unwarranted). The path resumes a W trend through dwarf mountain pines, soon passing the 1805m junction (30min, where n.803 turns off via Forcella di Scarnia for Vignui).

On a wider track, of military origin, you proceed in gentle ascent over karstic landscape featuring dolina depressions, and into the vast Costa Alpe Ramezza amphitheatre. A marked curve across scree cuts the middle of **Monte Ramezza** in a magnificent milieu. A grassy crest is gained (2050m) in the vicinity of an aerial, a rare landmark! From this angle the mountain's awesome face is revealed: infinite layers of creamy stone. Moreover, there are dizzy views to Fiera di Primiero and its valley,

STAGE 12 – RIFUGIO BOZ TO RIFUGIO DAL PIAZ

without forgetting the Pale di San Martino that dominate. A brief narrow stretch on the N of the ridge concludes with a drop down a grassy slope facing Cima del Diavolo as you head for Piazza del Diavolo to be dwarfed by flows of chaotic shattered rocks.

(A rusty pole marks a faint turn-off for a natural ice cave Giazzera di Ramezza, some 200m lower down, but only explorable with appropriate equipment. Inhabitants of Pedavena used to trek up here to cut block from a gigantic frozen cone for the town's brewery, especially during wartime when it was requisitioned.)

After a lovely stretch past Col Fontana is a stony-grassy bowl housing a ruined farm. Below Cima Dodici you bear SW over Busa di Pietena, which sports vast red slabs and curious piles of eroded rocks like giant's tiddlywinks. From **Passo Pietena** (2094m) a ridge stretches SE to Monte Pietena and collapsed wartime constructions are at hand. Ahead looms the bulk of Monte Pavione WSW.

The path curves S into magnificent Busa delle Vette, a veritable sea of karstic dolinas and grassed-over glacial mounds. Bells from the cows of the summer farm resound

Busa delle Vette is pitted with dolinas

across the basin, formerly known as Busa delle Meraviglie for its wealth of natural marvels including bright blue delphiniums and hawks hunting. You're joined by the jeep track from the farm for the gentle climb to **Passo delle Vette Grandi** (1994m). Only minutes down the other side, at last, is

3hr 20min – Rifugio Dal Piaz (1993m), named after a prominent geologist. ☎ 0439 9065, CAI, sleeps 24, open May to Nov, www.rifugiodalpiaz.it. Polenta comes with *funghi* (mushrooms) or *formaggio fuso* (melted cheese), both scrumptious. Then there are fragrant home-made cakes.

The outlook here is definitely non-dolomitic, but there are vast views across the Piave river plain and even views of the Adriatic coast and Venice are possible on a clear day. After dark the lowlands fill up with the twinkling lights of 'civilisation', your destination tomorrow.

STAGE 13
Rifugio Dal Piaz to Croce d'Aune

Time	1hr 30min
Distance	6km/3.7 miles
Descent	980m
Grade	2

A long leisurely descent on an old military road is followed by a good path through cool woodland, vast views and wildflowers galore adding to the fascination as the memorable AV2 draws near to its conclusion. Modest hotels, restaurants and cafés are available at the Croce d'Aune road pass (not to mention a bus service), where the AV2 comes to an end, like all good things must! The justifiably popular garden brewery of Pedavena awaits, as do more creature comforts and ongoing transport at the attractive Renaissance town of Feltre, which stands on the edge of the vast Veneto plain.

STAGE 13 – RIFUGIO DAL PIAZ TO CROCE D'AUNE

From **Rifugio Dal Piaz** (1993m) n.801 cuts S down grassed flanks onto an old military road that snakes its way down these impervious mountainsides with tight corners and plenty of short cuts. Rock faces host colonies of bear's-ear primrose saxifrage rosettes, while meadows are thick with pheasant's-eye narcissus. Great views can be enjoyed back to the massif atop imposing cliff barriers. The road drops on a rough and tiring stony stretch through wood, where mud can mean slippery going after rain. You end up on a minor surfaced road near a water trough close to houses. Continue R for a matter of minutes to

The old wartime track snaking its way downhill

1hr 30min – Passo di Croce d'Aune (1015m). Parco Nazionale delle Dolomiti Bellunesi Info Point, two hotel/restaurants (Albergo Croce d'Aune ☎ 0439 977000, www.crocedaune.it and Al Camoscio ☎ 0439 977058), as well as a café that sells Dolomiti Bus tickets for Feltre, a daily summertime service.

En route the bus passes through the pretty town of **Pedavena** (9km), home to an attractive, popular brewery

TREKKING IN THE DOLOMITES

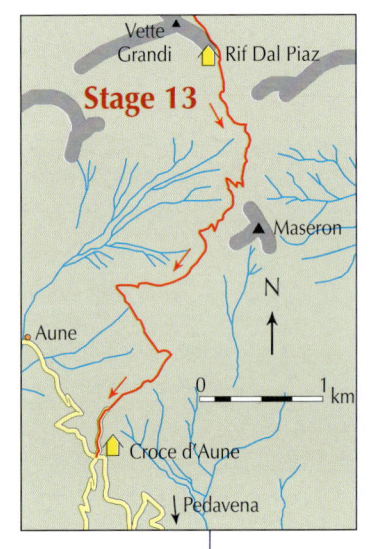

Stage 13

The lovely Renaissance town of Feltre

since 1896, www.labirreriapedavena. com. A great place to celebrate with a meal and beer in the relaxing, rambling gardens.

A further 3km on is beautiful **Feltre** (325m), a walled Renaissance town with frescoed houses, a modest museum and art gallery, well worth an exploratory wander. In August an exciting medieval Palio celebration is held and the whole town dresses up in costume. Remember to present your rifugi stamps at the Tourist Office for your AV2 badge (Piazzetta Trento e Trieste 9 ☏ 0439 2540).

Accommodation includes centrally located B&B Centro Storico ☎ 0439 81033 or ☎ cell 347 9609670, gio.bettega@tiscali.it. Trentino Trasporti buses run to Trento for rail connections back to Bressanone if needed, otherwise trains head S towards Treviso and Venice.

162

ALTE VIE 3–6

Rifugio Venezia dwarfed by the mighty Pelmo (AV3)

TREKKING IN THE DOLOMITES

ALTA VIA 3

Start	Villabassa
Finish	Longarone
Time	45hr – 8 days
Distance	100km
Highest point	2378m
Difficulty	Grade 2–3 with numerous short aided sections
Access	Villabassa in Val Pusteria is served by train and SAD bus; Longarone at the end has trains on the Venice–Calalzo line and Dolomiti Bus runs to Belluno.

The Alta Via dei Camosci ('chamois') commences by spending several particularly rewarding, drawn-out days rambling past the magnificent Cristallo and Sorapiss massifs. After veering over Val Biois near Cortina d'Ampezzo it touches on the mighty Pelmo and modest Monte Rite – a superb lookout. The rugged solitary Sfornoi-Bosconero group is traversed with a sequence of challenging exposed passages, mostly aided, before the trek conclusion at Longarone in the Piave valley – a key traffic artery. Overnight stays are in refuges and guesthouses, then in a spartan bivouac hut on the last night.

Beginning at **Villabassa** (1153m) near the railway station, AV3 strikes out on road at first across farmland and woods, preparing itself for a tiring series of ups and downs on very narrow paths over little-frequented ridges. Passing a smidgen below the summit of Picco di Vallandro, it reaches **Pratopiazza** (1991m, 7hr), where wonderful meadows look over to Croda Rossa. Rifugio Pratopiazza ☎ 0474 748650, www.plaetzwiese.com; Hotel Hohe Gaisl ☎ 0474 748606, www.hohegaisl.com. Further on, and brilliantly placed for admiring sunsets on the Cristallo, is Rifugio Vallandro (2040m, 30min)

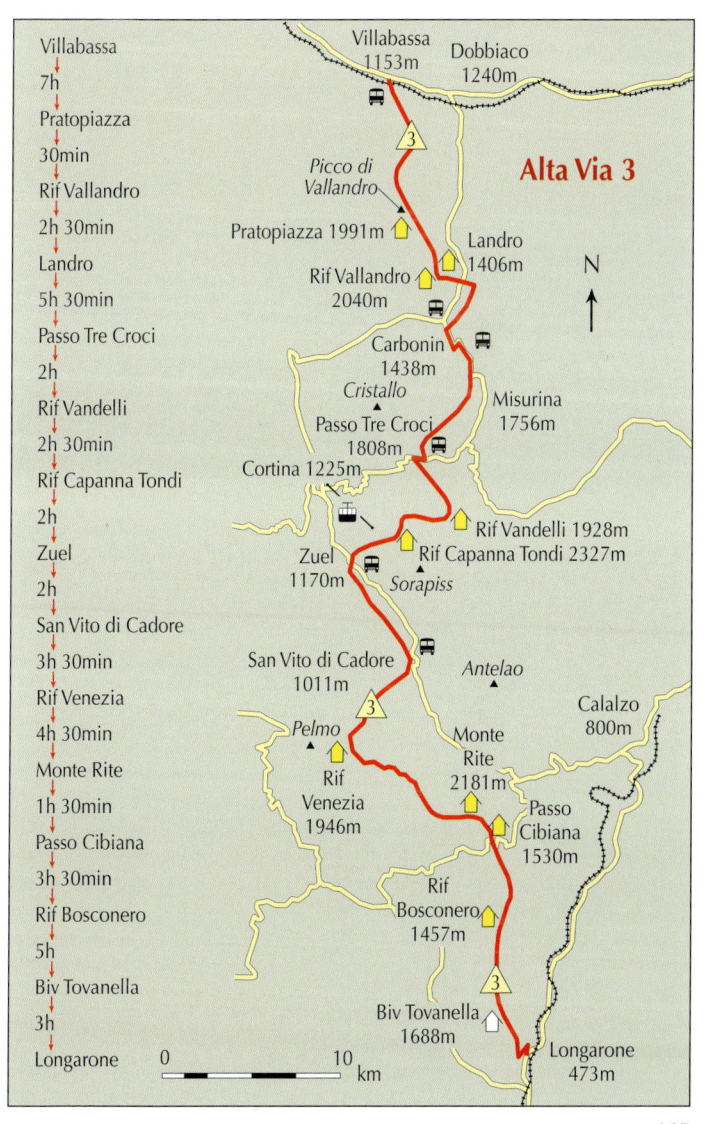

Alta Via 3

Itinerary	Map labels
Villabassa	Villabassa 1153m
7h	Dobbiaco 1240m
Pratopiazza	Picco di Vallandro
30min	Pratopiazza 1991m
Rif Vallandro	Landro 1406m
2h 30min	Rif Vallandro 2040m
Landro	Carbonin 1438m
5h 30min	Cristallo
Passo Tre Croci	Passo Tre Croci 1808m
2h	Misurina 1756m
Rif Vandelli	Cortina 1225m
2h 30min	Rif Vandelli 1928m
Rif Capanna Tondi	Rif Capanna Tondi 2327m
2h	Zuel 1170m
Zuel	Sorapiss
2h	San Vito di Cadore 1011m
San Vito di Cadore	Antelao
3h 30min	Calalzo 800m
Rif Venezia	Pelmo
4h 30min	Rif Venezia 1946m
Monte Rite	Monte Rite 2181m
1h 30min	Passo Cibiana 1530m
Passo Cibiana	Rif Bosconero 1457m
3h 30min	Biv Tovanella 1688m
Rif Bosconero	Longarone 473m
5h	
Biv Tovanella	
3h	
Longarone	

The Cristallo across from Rifugio Vallandro

☎ 0474 972505, www.vallandro.it. After climbing to a saddle close to Monte Specie, AV3 plunges helter-skelter to the valley floor at **Landro** (1406m, 2hr 30min), with accommodation at Hotel Drei Zinnen ☎ 0474 972633, www.hoteltrecime.com.

(A SAD bus can be picked up here to Misurina where a change is necessary to Dolomiti Bus for Passo Tre Croci). Now a broad track (a former railway) leads past Lago di Landro to **Carbonin** (1438m). A short distance up the Misurina road, a branch along Val Popena Alta that becomes a tiring climb to spectacularly located – but unfortunately ruined – Rifugio Popena (2214m). From an adjoining saddle an initially eroded tract makes its gradual way to the road and on to **Passo Tre Croci** (1808m, 5hr 30min).

A leisurely track cuts across the fossil-studded flanks of Cime Marcoira to a beautiful amphitheatre with a pretty turquoise lake in the shadow of the Sorapiss, and **Rifugio Vandelli** (1928m, 2hr) ☎ 0435 39015, CAI, 20 June to 20 Sept, www.rifugiovandelli.it.

Now a series of aided passages climbs to Forcella Ciadin (2378m), the highest point reached on the trek. A lovely traverse with vast views over the Cortina Dolomites reaches **Rifugio Capanna Tondi** (2327m, 2hr 30min) ☎ 0436 5775, mid-June to mid-Sept, tondillo@libero.it. Not far downhill is the cable-car to Cortina and Rifugio Faloria (☎ 0436 2737) but AV3 drops down Val Orita on a steep path into wood. This concludes at **Zuel** (1170m, 2hr) and the main road where a Dolomiti Bus can be caught to San Vito di Cadore. However, 'purists' will cross the road and head for Socol, where a track continues on the other side of Torrente Boite, ending up in the spread-out resort of **San Vito di Cadore** (1010m, 2hr) with hotels and shops.

On surfaced road as far as Serdes, AV3 then follows a jeep track that ascends relentlessly through wood, finally emerging to flowered meadows and **Rifugio Venezia** (1946m, 3hr 30min) ☎ 0436 9684, CAI, 20 June to 20 Sept. It stands at the foot of the throne of the gods, breathtaking Pelmo.

With a decisive swing around Monte Pena by way of minor saddles, a lane is joined to Rifugio Talamini (1582m, currently closed), before gaining height on a

The Sorapiss from Zuel

traverse to **Monte Rite** (2160m, 4hr 30min). Here a First World War fort has been converted into a museum and Rifugio Dolomites ☎ 0435 31315, June to Nov, www.rifugiomonterite.it. A winding 7km former military road – covered either on foot or by taking advantage of the shuttle bus – terminates at **Passo Cibiana** (1530m, 1hr 30min) and Rifugio Remauro ☎ 0435 74187, www.rifugioremauro.it, as well as Baita Deona ☎ 0435 540169, www.baitadeona.it.

Through a clutch of old 'tabià' huts it's a steady ascent to Forcella de le Ciavazole (1994m) in the rugged Sfornoi group, thence a knee-testing descent across vast scree spreads to **Rifugio Bosconero** (1457m, 3hr 30min) ☎ 0437 787346, CAI, 20 June to 20 Sept. ◀

> Anyone not in possession of the necessary equipment, food, experience or time needed for the following two days should bail out here – a path drops to Val Zoldana and Dolomiti bus runs to Longarone.

It's steep going beneath Sasso di Bosconero towards Forcella de la Tovanella (2150m), along jagged ridges over wild Val Tovanella with a series of tricky passages and narrow ledges. Intrepid chamois hunters forged these routes. After Forcella di Viàz de le Ponte (1909m) and guiding chains down a chimney, immense scree basin Vant de la Serra is crossed with a difficult exposed ledge and a hands-on scramble. Immediately after Porta de la Serra (2050m) is a plaque in memory of Brovelli and Tolot, who invented the AV3. Easier terrain is encountered down to converted herders' hut **Bivacco Tovanella** (1688m, 5hr), which has a tank of rainwater on the premises.

Following an initial climb to 1840m, straightforward paths continue high over Val del Maé, with vast outlooks and a string of old huts. Steady descent brings walkers to a surfaced road near the village of Podenzoi (799m). A final hour downhill means the conclusion of AV3 at **Longarone** (473m, 3hr) and a well-deserved cool drink at one of the hotels or restaurants here. The town is renowned for its creamy gelato – but also for the Vajont dam tragedy in 1963.

ALTA VIA 4

Start	San Candido
Finish	Pieve di Cadore
Time	33hr – 6 days
Distance	85km
Highest point	2624m
Difficulty	Grade 2–3 with long, exposed aided sections and vie ferrate, **which requires specialist equipment**
Access	San Candido in Val Pusteria has trains and SAD buses; at the other end Pieve di Cadore has Dolomiti Bus runs to Calalzo (trains), Cortina and Belluno.

Invented in 1973 by Toni Sanmarchi (along with AV5), AV4 was subtitled the 'Alta Via di Paul Grohmann' for the Viennese mountaineer who first scaled, amongst others, the Tre Scarperi, Cima Grande di Lavaredo, Sorapiss and Antelao, all of which punctuate the route. AV4 begins its wonderful trans-Dolomite journey in the spectacular Sesto group with good paths, a host of breathtaking vistas and a string of popular refuges. Then airy aided ways take over, threading through the Cadini line-up of spires. Opposite are the rugged Marmarole, explored on lengthy but thrilling aided scrambles where experience is a must. The trek wraps up with a wander round the middle of soaring Antelao, before descending to the elegant alpine township of Pieve di Cadore. Overnight stays are in well-run refuges and one tiny bivouac hut.

From historic **San Candido** (1174m) cover the 4km to Alte Säge (45min), either by lane or SAD bus. Here AV3 penetrates the Sesto Dolomites by way of Val Campo di Dentro. (A midsummer shuttle runs part way up.) Wood and meadows accompany to **Rifugio Tre Scarperi** (1626m, 2hr)

Via ferrata gear and experience are essential for the Cadini and Marmarole sections.

Trekking in the Dolomites

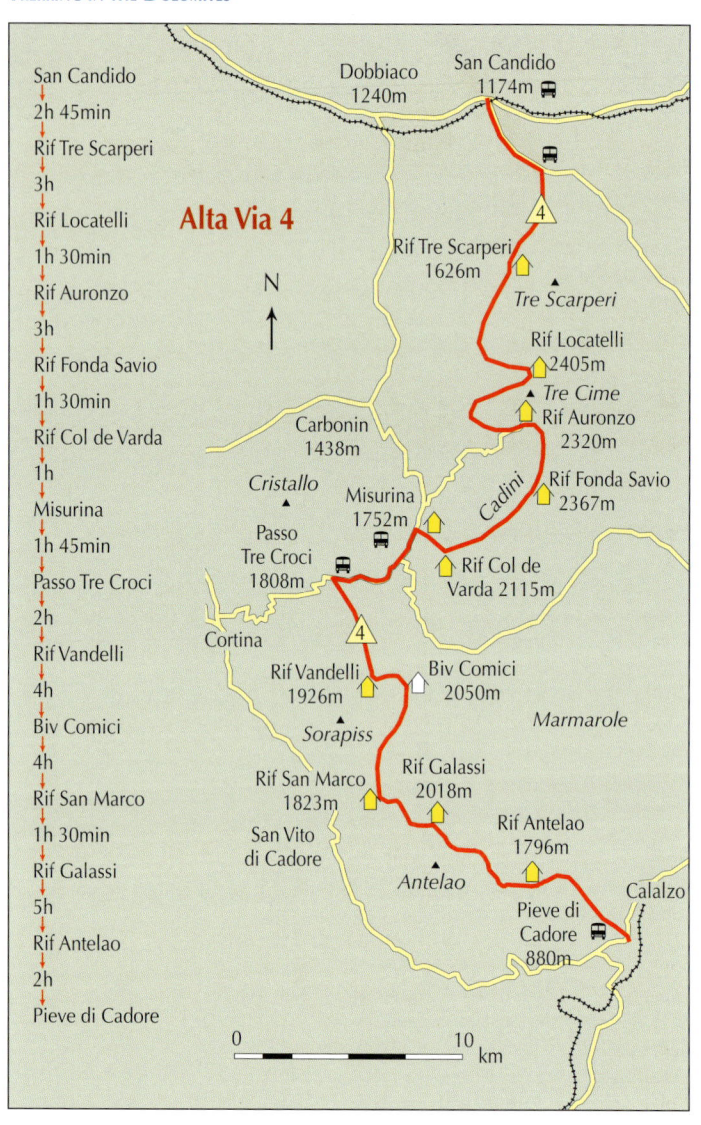

Alta Via 4

San Candido
↓ 2h 45min
Rif Tre Scarperi
↓ 3h
Rif Locatelli
↓ 1h 30min
Rif Auronzo
↓ 3h
Rif Fonda Savio
↓ 1h 30min
Rif Col de Varda
↓ 1h
Misurina
↓ 1h 45min
Passo Tre Croci
↓ 2h
Rif Vandelli
↓ 4h
Biv Comici
↓ 4h
Rif San Marco
↓ 1h 30min
Rif Galassi
↓ 5h
Rif Antelao
↓ 2h
Pieve di Cadore

170

Alta Via 4

Crossing the Sesto group

☎ 0474 966610, CAI, June to Nov, www.drei-schuster-huette.com, where Tyrolean specialities are the order of the day.

Clear paths climb beneath a stunning line-up of peaks to the upland to see the magnificent Tre Cime di Lavaredo from **Rifugio Locatelli** (2405m, 3hr) ☎ 0474 972002, CAI, June to Oct dreizinnenhuette@rolmail.net. An old wartime mule track circles around the magnificent three via Col di Mezzo (2324m) to a road and **Rifugio Auronzo** (2320m, 1hr 30min) ☎ 0435 39002, CAI, June to Sept, www.rifugioauronzo.it. SAD and Dolomiti Bus services to Misurina and beyond.

Maintaining altitude, AV4 now follows Sentiero Bonacossa, a WW1 route along the central ridge of the Cadini dodging elegant rock needles. Cables, ladders, rungs, ledges and a tunnel lead to Forcella de Rinbianco (2176m) and under Torre Wundt around to **Rifugio Fondo Savio** (2367m, 3hr) ☎ 0435 39036, CAI, 15 June to 15 Sept. In a similar vein the path continues in the direction of an imposing tower to Forcella del Diavolo (2598m) and across the Ciadin de la Neve snowfield. More aided passages cross rubble gullies, thence a good path to **Rifugio Col de Varda** (2115m, 1hr 30min), ☎ 0435 39041, June

Trekking in the Dolomites

Rifugio Fondo Savio

to Sept, www.rifugiocoldevarda.it. Either follow the lane or ride the chair lift to **Misurina** (1752m, 1hr; hotels, groceries) where a beautiful lake reflects majestic peaks. Take a Dolomiti Bus for the 6km journey to **Passo Tre Croci** (1808m) or allow 1hr 45min on foot along the road.

In common with AV3, a leisurely track cuts beneath Cime Marcoira to a stunning amphitheatre with a pretty turquoise lake, and **Rifugio Vandelli** (1926m, 2hr) ☎ 0435 39015, CAI, 20 June to 20 Sept, www.rifugiovandelli.it. ▶

The breathtaking Sorapiss towers overhead.

Curving high over Val d'Ansiei full-blooded via ferrata Vandelli is fitted with ladders, rungs and cable on an exciting climb to 2370m over Col del Fuoco via chimneys, ledges and sheer rock faces. Shrubby vegetation and grass reappear in Busa del Banco, then it's a drop via steep flanks to **Bivacco Comici** (2050, 4hr).

Dizzy over Val di San Vito, the Sentiero Minazio means more aided exposed passages and difficulty en route to magnificent Forcella Grande (2255m) under amazing Torre Sabbioni, and down to welcoming **Rifugio San Marco** (1823m, 4hr), ☎ 0436 9444, CAI, 20 June to 20 Sept, www.rifugiosanmarco.com (exit path to San Vito di Cadore.) Over eroding terrain, a clear path cuts across to Forcella Piccola (2120m) and the converted barracks **Rifugio Galassi** (2018m, 1hr 30min) ☎ 0436 9685, CAI, June to Sept, rifugiogalassi@caimestre.it.

In the shadow of giant pyramidal Antelao, AV4 proceeds over tiring moraine and a rock face up to Forcella del Ghiacciaio (2584m), to the sight of ice domes on the shrinking glacier. A steep, tricky chimney drops to grass and light wood in Val Antelao. Once Forcella Piria (2096m) is gained, with vast views to the Duranno-Cima dei Preti groups, it's easy going past the Crode di San Pietro and on to **Rifugio Antelao** (1796m, 5hr) ☎ 0435 75333, CAI, June to Oct, www.rifugio-antelao.it.

A jeep track leads via Forcella Antracisa (1693m), where it's best to avoid Monte Tranego and choose the path to Pozzale (1054m). There, either by Dolomiti Bus or along the road, cover the remaining 1.6km to **Pieve di Cadore** (880m, 2hr) for hotels, restaurants and transport.

ALTA VIA 5

Start	Sesto
Finish	Pieve di Cadore
Time	38hr – 7 days
Distance	90km
Highest point	2650m
Difficulty	Grade 2–3 with extended exposed and aided sections, vie ferrate **(require specialist equipment)**
Access	Sesto, in an eastern branch of Val Pusteria, is served by SAD buses; at the other end Pieve di Cadore has Dolomiti Bus runs to Calalzo (trains) and Belluno.

Running parallel to AV4, this trek similarly concludes at Pieve di Cadore – birthplace of Renaissance artist Titian, who immortalised these landscapes in his canvases, hence the dedication Alta Via di Tiziano. After traversing the magnificent and popular Sesto Dolomites with comfortable refuges, AV5 drops across the Auronzo valley to embark on an arduous, solitary and highly rewarding exploration of the wild Marmarole range. This means a sequence of tough interlinked aided routes and bivouac huts, with the occasional manned refuge. **Bottom line** Take sleeping, cooking and full via ferrata gear. **Note** Water is scarce.

From **Sesto** (1302m) on foot it's 3km to the opening of beautiful Val Fiscalina and **Dolomitenhof** (1454m, 30min), but SAD buses also run this far. Through flowered meadows flanking the mammoth Tre Scarperi, a lane quickly reaches **Rifugio Fondo Valle** (1548m) ☎ 0474 710606 May to Oct, www.talschlusshuette.com. With a vast choice of dramatic mountains to admire, AV5 climbs steadily to **Rifugio Zsigmondy-Comici** (2224m, 2hr) ☎ 0474 710358, CAI, June to Oct, magnificently located opposite Monte Popera.

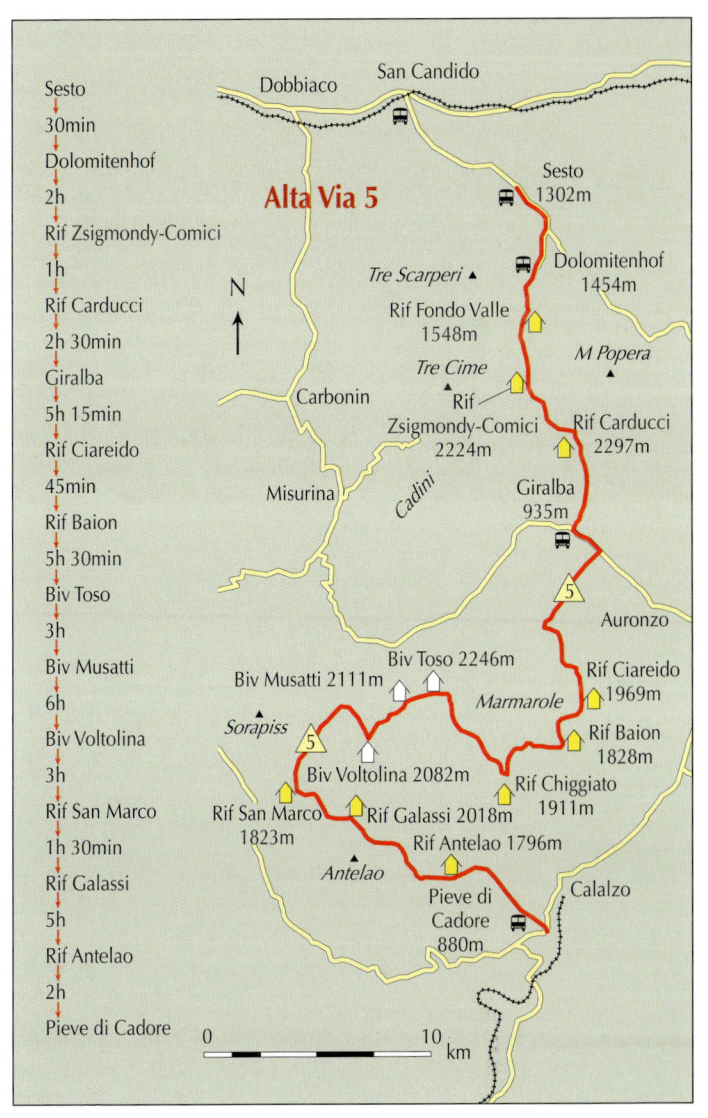

ALTA VIA 5

Sesto
↓ 30min
Dolomitenhof
↓ 2h
Rif Zsigmondy-Comici
↓ 1h
Rif Carducci
↓ 2h 30min
Giralba
↓ 5h 15min
Rif Ciareido
↓ 45min
Rif Baion
↓ 5h 30min
Biv Toso
↓ 3h
Biv Musatti
↓ 6h
Biv Voltolina
↓ 3h
Rif San Marco
↓ 1h 30min
Rif Galassi
↓ 5h
Rif Antelao
↓ 2h
Pieve di Cadore

Alta Via 5

Dobbiaco — San Candido — Sesto 1302m — Dolomitenhof 1454m — *Tre Scarperi* — Rif Fondo Valle 1548m — *M Popera* — *Tre Cime* — Rif Zsigmondy-Comici 2224m — Rif Carducci 2297m — Carbonin — Giralba 935m — Misurina — *Cadini* — Auronzo — Rif Ciareido 1969m — Biv Musatti 2111m — Biv Toso 2246m — *Marmarole* — Rif Baion 1828m — *Sorapiss* — Biv Voltolina 2082m — Rif Chiggiato 1911m — Rif San Marco 1823m — Rif Galassi 2018m — Rif Antelao 1796m — *Antelao* — Pieve di Cadore 880m — Calalzo

0 — 10 km

Aided stretch en route to Forcella Sacu

6km away by Dolomiti Bus is lakeside Auronzo (866m) with hotels, restaurants and groceries.

The scree-filled head of Val Fiscalina Alta is traversed to Forcella Giralba (2431m), thence quiet **Rifugio Carducci** (2297m, 1hr) ☎ 0435 400485, CAI, June to Oct, www.rifugiocarducci.eu.

A long tiring descent ensues alongside an ice-blue torrent and through wood dwarfed by soaring rock walls. The path emerges on the road at **Giralba** (935m, 2hr 30min). ◄ It's only a couple of km downstream to Orsolina where the Torrente Ansiei is crossed and a minor road leads up pastoral Valle da Rin to café-eatery La Primula (1060m, 1hr 15min). Heading decidedly uphill to cut across the easternmost corner of the Marmarole, AV5 climbs an eroded gully to panoramic Forcella Paradiso (2045m), thence cosy **Rifugio Ciareido** (1969m, 4hr) ☎ 0435 76276, May to Oct, www.rifugiociareido.com. A straightforward path through a sea of dwarf mountain pines goes to **Rifugio Baion** (1828m, 45min) ☎ 0435 76060, CAI, June to Sept, www.rifugiobaion.it.

Skirting rugged mounts aided by short stretches of cable, Forcella Sacu (1914m, 2hr) is reached in

Alta Via 5

a clearing. (Only a 20min detour away is **Rifugio Chiggiato** (1911m) ☎ 0435 31452, CAI, 20 June to 20 Sept). Soon AV5 becomes vertical and joins a via ferrata with lengths of cable to Forcella Jau de la Tana (2650m) and brilliant views. This leads down into the hidden world of the Lastoni delle Marmarole, vast eroded rock slabs where orientation can be tricky in low visibility. Well looked-after metal cabin **Bivacco Toso** (2246m, 3hr 30min) stands alongside historic stone Rifugio Tiziano (locked). ▶

Water can be found 30min downhill.

A faint route ascends Val Longa, making its way up the Tacco del Todesco ridge. Hands-on and aided ledge passages lead to a 2614m saddle with a brilliant outlook. A bit more clambering on the 'Strada Sanmarchi' concludes in desolate Meduce di Fuori where snow lies late, and **Bivacco Musatti** (2111m, 3hr), another essential metallic structure.

Especially difficult and tiring climbing passages come next, on the approach to Forcella del Mescol (2400m), and across the head of Meduce di Dentro, a solitary cirque. Ladders and a precious water source are encountered on

The Marmarole line-up

177

Rifugio San Marco

the approach to unworldly Forcella di Croda Rotta (2569m). A challenging narrow crest and ledges lead to dizzy Forcella Vanedel (2372m). Further aided sections with cable round the Croda de Marchi and more ledge. From a stream (alias water supply), it's not far to **Bivacco Voltolina** (2082m, 6hr) in vast amphitheatre Van di Scotter.

The Corno del Doge is rounded on a continuous exposed natural ledge, with the help of cable. With several tricky points, it gradually joins a path in Val di San Vito, then climbs in the shade of Torre Sabbioni to reach Forcella Grande (2255m). It's down to welcoming **Rifugio San Marco** (1823m, 3hr) ☎ 0436 9444, CAI, 20 June to 20 Sept, www.rifugiosanmarco.com.

From here on the trek is in common with AV4 – see above. This entails 1hr 30min to **Rifugio Galassi** (2018m), a further 5hr to **Rifugio Antelao** (1796m) and concluding 2hr to **Pieve di Cadore** (880m).

ALTA VIA 6

Start	Rifugio Sorgenti del Piave (Sappada)
Finish	Vittorio Veneto
Time	65 hr – 11 days
Distance	180km
Highest point	2450m
Difficulty	Grade 2–3 with long exposed sections, some aided, and difficult terrain where orientation can be a problem
Access	The closest bus stop is Cima Sappada (1236m), reachable by Dolomiti Bus from Calalzo (trains) and SAF runs from Tolmezzo. Allow an extra 3hr for the 6km up Val Sesis on paths and a little tarmac. Vittorio Veneto at the trek finish is on the Venice-Calalzo train line.

Fascinating, if protracted, 'Alta Via dei Silenzi' explores the spectacular little-trodden eastern fringe of the Dolomites. Beginning at the source of the Piave, it runs parallel to the important river valley. Gently paced opening days cross the Cridola, Spalti di Toro-Monfalconi groups with a decent scatter of refuges. Next AV6 tramps through the rugged Duranno-Cima dei Preti where paths become fainter and accommodation spartan. The going can be harsh. After Erto is less dramatic, medium-altitude Col Nudo-Cavallo and fair distances along asphalted road. It goes without saying that walkers must be fit, experienced, self-sufficient and well equipped.

The AV6 starts officially at Sorgenti del Piave but Rifugio Calvi (2164m) (☎ 0435 9232, CAI, June to Oct) on beautiful Peralba – 1hr 30min return – is well worth a visit if you have extra time.

TREKKING IN THE DOLOMITES

From **Rifugio Sorgenti del Piave** (1815m) (☎ 0435 469260, June to Sept) a panoramic path climbs over gullies leading to Passo del Mulo (2356m) surrounded by trenches and reminders of WW1. Well below the clutch of tarns Laghi d'Olbe (2156m) is Ristorante Gosse (1847m, 3hr) where linked chair lifts glide downhill, an alternative to a monotonous jeep track to charming spread-out **Sappada** (1240m, 1hr 30min on foot). Groceries can be bought here, while hotels include Pensione Fontana ☎ 0435 469174, pensionefontana@libero.it.

From Granvilla AV6 ventures along the wooded Enghe valley, branching off via waterfalls to Passo Elbel (1963m). A traverse high over Val Pesarina entails eroded passages via the Clap Piccolo clearing (1623m) before approaching Clap Grande and **Rifugio Fratelli De Gasperi** (1767m, 4h 30min) ☎ 0433 69069, CAI, June to Sept.

The route backtracks to Clap Piccolo for a long gradual descent via Forcella Lavardet (1491m). Quiet surfaced roads and lanes lead up and down through wood and meadow, finally gaining friendly **Rifugio Fabbro** (1783m, 4hr) ☎ 0435 460357, www.rifugiofabbro.it, facing Monte Tudaio.

The graceful Peralba rises above woodland

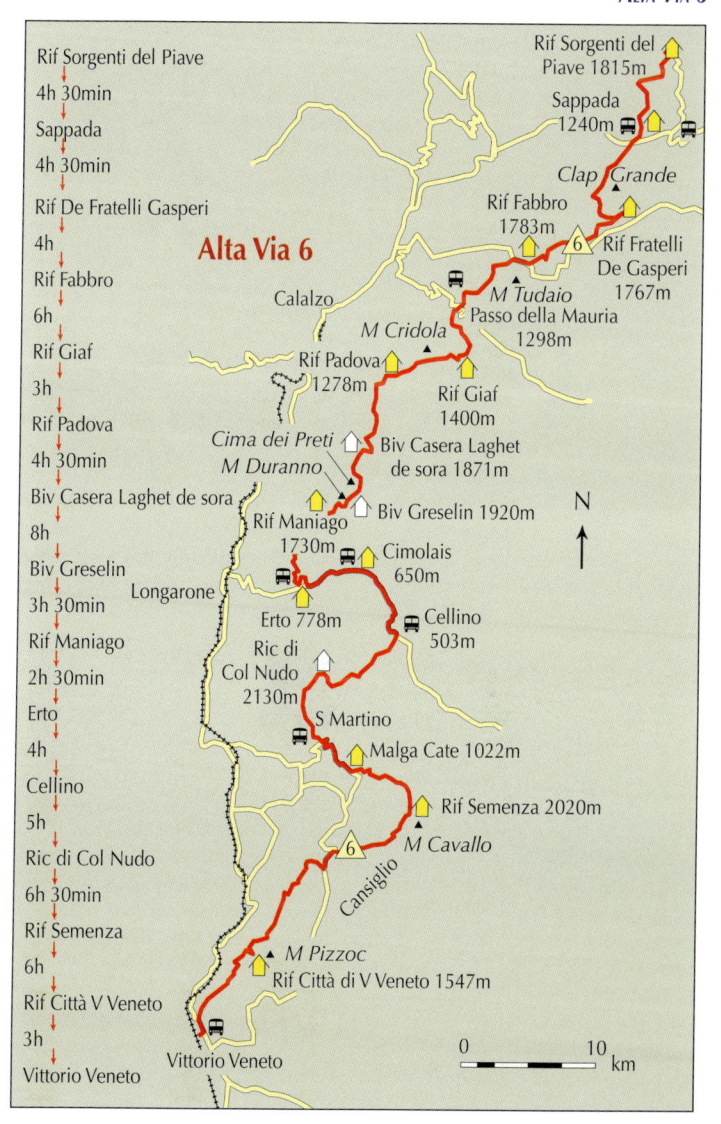

Alta Via 6

Rif Sorgenti del Piave

4h 30min

Sappada

4h 30min

Rif De Fratelli Gasperi

4h

Rif Fabbro

6h

Rif Giaf

3h

Rif Padova

4h 30min

Biv Casera Laghet de sora

8h

Biv Greselin

3h 30min

Rif Maniago

2h 30min

Erto

4h

Cellino

5h

Ric di Col Nudo

6h 30min

Rif Semenza

6h

Rif Città V Veneto

3h

Vittorio Veneto

Rif Sorgenti del Piave 1815m
Sappada 1240m
Clap Grande
Rif Fabbro 1783m
Rif Fratelli De Gasperi 1767m
Calalzo
M Tudaio
Passo della Mauria 1298m
M Cridola
Rif Padova 1278m
Rif Giaf 1400m
Cima dei Preti
M Duranno
Biv Casera Laghet de sora 1871m
Rif Maniago 1730m
Biv Greselin 1920m
Cimolais 650m
Longarone
Erto 778m
Cellino 503m
Ric di Col Nudo 2130m
S Martino
Malga Cate 1022m
Rif Semenza 2020m
M Cavallo
Cansiglio
M Pizzoc
Rif Città di V Veneto 1547m
Vittorio Veneto

N ↑

0   10 km

TREKKING IN THE DOLOMITES

Rifugio Giaf

By all means exit here to Calalzo and the railway station if you're not equipped for the tougher stuff that follows.

A 3km stretch of tarmac and AV6 heads along a lane to scenically placed Casera Doana (1911m). Cutting over Col Rosolo on forest pathways it veers sharply over Alta Val del Tagliamento, joining a lane to **Passo della Mauria** (1298m, 4hr). As well as a café-restaurant, the road pass has SAF buses going in both directions – via Calalzo to Pieve di Cadore, or to Tolmezzo.

A lane breaks off, soon becoming a path through wood, open mountainsides and over streams on a roller coaster route to **Rifugio Giaf** (1400m, 2hr) ☎ 0433 88002, CAI, June to Sept, www.rifugiogiaf.it.

A steady ascent into inspirational rockscapes and a cirque reaches Forcella Scodavacca (2043m) under Monte Cridola, for a breather before the plunge to the Pra' de Toro meadows and cosy **Rifugio Padova** (1278m, 3hr) ☎ 0435 72488, CAI, May to Oct, www. rifugiopadova.it. ◄

AV6 climbs through wood over Torrente Talagona to a 1360m fork, thence up steep Fosso degli Elmi. Superb rocky crest outlines of the Spalti di Toro appear en route to Forcella Spè (2049m, 3hr) the gateway to

Val Cimoliana. ▶ Rugged Val Misera and Valle dei Lares are crossed in quick succession, before an outcrop is rounded to Val dei Frassin where lovely **Bivacco Casera Laghet de sora** (1871m, 1hr 30min) stands in a veritable botanical garden with water nearby.

With scarce waymarks a path flanks Cima Laste heading into a vast amphitheatre en route to Forcella Val dei Drap (2290m, 2hr). A steep drop to Forcella dei Cacciatori (2173m) soon becomes a hands-on stretch along the flanks of Cima dei Preti. Val dei Cantoni is crossed and there's more rock climbing to Forcella Compol (2450m, 4hr). A long downhill section into a gully includes tricky passages, before a snowfield is crossed. Further on is a difficult ledge requiring acrobatic skill. Further on still, after a shoulder is rounded, is **Bivacco Greselin** (1920m, 2hr), in a wonderful cirque overshadowed by Cima dei Frati. Spring water can be found nearby.

It's not far up to a gully that needs to be ascended with the help of cables, followed by exposed ledges and clambers as AV6 moves across difficult terrain towards Monte Duranno. After a cave the next landmark is Forcella Duranno (2217m), before a descent over rock and into the trees to homely **Rifugio Maniago** (1730m, 3hr 30min) ☎ 0427 879144, CAI, June to Sept.

It's easy walking down to the rough road in Val Zemola, which leads to the village of **Erto** (778m, 2hr 30min), sadly involved in the 1963 Vajont disaster when neighbouring Monte Toc slid into a dam, generating a gigantic destructive wave; B&B ☎ 333 4140830 or Hotel Erto ☎ 0427 879053, www.hotelerto.com. To exit here, the ATAP bus can be taken to Longarone (12km) for trains. Otherwise, in the opposite direction, it runs via Cimolais (650m, plenty of accommodation) for a change to **Cellino** (503m), a saving of approximately 4hr for the 13.5km.

Valle Chialedina leads towards woodland and Col Nudo, gaining height all of a sudden. Rock steps and cable lead up to the crest and Passo di Valbona (2130m, 5hr) with **Ricovero di Col Nudo**, an atmospheric cave fitted out as a bivouac shelter; water is available inside.

Bivacco Gervasutti is close by

Rifugio Padova

Past curious sculpted outcrops, AV6 heads downhill to Scalet Bassa (1169m) and surfaced road, in the Alpago district now. By way of Casera Stabali, San Martino (bus to Belluno) and Funes (817m), it reaches Tamera (914m) for a short cut joining a final stretch of road to **Malga Cate** (1022m, 2hr 30min) ☎ cell 328 8787012, a cosy converted farm with rooms and meals.

Close by a track heads along karstic Val Salatis, then Valle Sperlonga to Forcella Laste on Monte Cavallo and scenically placed **Rifugio Semenza** (2020m, 4hr) ☎ 0437 49055, CAI, June to Sept, www.caivv.it/rifugiosemenza.

A panoramic path through a cirque ends at Casera Palatina (1521m) thence good paths to Canaie and Val Tritton, to a short stretch of tarmac to Campon (1040m, bus, 1hr 30min). Here a road closed to traffic curves around to Palughetto for a lane in ascent through wood to Col Mazzuc and across to the panoramic crest high over the Cansiglio forest and pastoral basin. Across Pian de la Pita and past Monte Millifret, the Casere Pizzoc turn-off (1499m) is finally reached – it's a short worthwhile detour to Monte Pizzoc and rambling **Rifugio Città di Vittorio Veneto** (1547m, 4hr 30min) ☎ cell 368 3708978, May to Sept.

Back at the turn-off begins the long gradual descent by way of Agnelezza, then a lane to a small quarry. A path along wooded Costa di Serravalle drops to the chapel of Sant'Augusta (350m) for a paved lane into Serravalle, the charming Renaissance part of **Vittorio Veneto** (139m, 3hr). Plenty of hotels, restaurants, cafés, as well as trains and buses, are only a short stroll away.

APPENDIX A
Glossary

The following terms are mostly in Italian; German terms are denoted (G)

acqua (non) potabile	water (not) suitable for drinking	capitello	shrine
agriturismo	farm with meals and/or accommodation	carta escursionistica	walking map
		cascata	waterfall
aiuto!	help!	casera	hut
albergo	hotel	caserma	barracks
alimentari	grocery shop	castello	castle
alpe	mountain pasture	cengia	ledge
alta via	high level mountain route	cima	mountain summit
alto	high	col	hill, mountain or saddle
altopiano/altipiano	high altitude plateau, upland	corda metallica	metal cable on aided route
aperto/chiuso	open/closed	croce	cross
autostazione	bus station	croda	steep-sided mountain
autostrada	toll-paying motorway	cuccetta	bunk bed
bagno	bathroom or toilet	custode	hut guardian
baita	alpine shepherd's hut, sometimes a farm or refuge	destra/sinistra	right/left
		difficile	difficult
		diga	dam
basso	low	discesa/salita	descent/ascent
bivacco	bivouac hut, unmanned	doccia fredda/calda	cold/hot shower
bosco	wood	est, orientale	east
burrone	ravine	facile	easy
bus, busa	Belluno district name for a glacially-formed cirque	fermata dell'autobus	bus stop
		fiume	river
cabinovia, telecabina	gondola car lift	fontana	fountain
caduta sassi	rock falls	forcella	saddle, pass
campanile	rock spire (lit. 'bell tower')	funivia	cable-car
		galleria	tunnel
campeggio	camping, camping ground	gettone	token for a shower in the huts
capanna	hut	ghiacciaio	glacier

185

TREKKING IN THE DOLOMITES

giro	tour	*rio, torrente*	mountain stream
grande	large	*ristoro*	refreshments
grotta	cave	*rotabile*	motorable road
Höhenweg (G)	high-level mountain route	*sasso*	boulder or rocky peak
Hütte (G)	manned mountain hut	*scarpone*	hiking boot
Jausenstation (G)	alpine café, refreshment point	*Scharte (G)*	pass, col
		scorciatoia	short cut
Lager (G)	dormitory	*seggiovia*	chair lift
lago	lake	*Seilbahn (G)*	gondola or cable-car
malga	mountain farm, sometimes a refuge	*sella*	saddle
		sentiero	path
meteo, previsioni del tempo	weather forecast	*sentiero alpinistico/ attrezzato*	climbing/aided route
mezzo	middle	*soccorso alpino*	mountain rescue
molino, mulino	mill	*sorgente*	spring (water)
monte	mountain	*spiz*	rock point, peak
nevaio	snow field	*stazione ferroviaria*	railway station
nord, settentrionale	north	*strada*	road
nuovo percorso	new routing	*sud, meridionale*	south
ometto	cairn, lit. 'little man'	*tabià*	haymaking chalet
orario	timetable	*tappa*	stage
orrido	ravine	*teleferica*	aerial cableway
ovest, occidente	west	*telefono*	telephone
pala	a rounded, spade-shaped mountain	*torre*	tower
		torrente	mountain stream
panificio	bakery	*val, valle, vallone*	valley
passo	mountain pass or saddle	*vedretta*	hanging glacier
percorso alpinistico/ attrezzato	climbing/aided route	*vetta*	peak
		via ferrata	aided climbing route
pericolo	danger	*via normale*	normal ascent route for climbers
pian	level ground		
piccolo	small	*Weg (G)*	route, way
ponte	bridge		
pronto soccorso	first aid		
punta	mountain peak		
ricovero invernale	winter shelter adjoining a refuge		
rifugio	manned mountain hut		

APPENDIX B
Route Summary Tables

Alta Via 1

Stage	From	To	Time	Distance	Ascent/Descent	Grade
1	Lago di Braies	Rifugio Biella	3hr	6.5km	870m/60m	2
2	Rifugio Biella	Rifugio Fanes	4hr 30	13.5km	630m/870m	1
3	Rifugio Fanes	Rifudio Lagazuoi	5hr 30	12km	1150m/450m	2
4	Rifugio Lagazuoi	Rifugio Nuvolau	5hr	14km	900m/1080m	2
5	Rifugio Nuvolau	Rifugio Città di Fiume	5hr 10	12km	400m/1050m	2–3
6	Rifugio Città di Fiume	Rifugio Coldai	3hr 40	9.3km	520m/300m	2
7	Rifugio Coldai	Rifugio Vazzoler	3hr 45	9.5km	380m/800m	2
8	Rifugio Vazzoler	Rifugio Carestiato	3hr 20	9km	600m/480m	2+
9	Rifugio Carestiato	Rifugio Pramperet	4hr 20	13km	550m/530m	2
10	Rifugio Pramperet	Rifugio Pian de Fontana	3hr	6.4km	540m/760m	2–3
11	Rifugio Pian de Fontana	La Pissa bus stop	3hr 45	13km	120m/1300m	2

Alta Via 2

Stage	From	To	Time	Distance	Ascent/Descent	Grade
1	Bressanone	Rifugio Città di Bressanone	5hr 30	11km	1900m/–	2
2	Rifugio Città di Bressanone	Rifugio Genova	4hr	13km	610m/760m	2
3	Rifugio Genova	Rifugio Puez	5hr	12km	820m/645m	2–3
4	Rifugio Puez	Rifugio Pisciadù	5hr	9km	660m/550m	3
5	Rifugio Pisciadù	Rifugio Castiglioni	6hr 30	14.5km	710m/1250m	3
6	Rifugio Castiglioni	Passo San Pellegrino	7hr	21.5km	1110m/1240m	2
7	Passo San Pellegrino	Rifugio Mulaz	5hr 15	13km	1346m/708m	3
8	Rifugio Mulaz	Rifugio Rosetta	4hr 15	8km	860m/850m	3+
9	Rifugio Rosetta	Rifugio Treviso	6hr 15	14km	820m/1770m	3
10	Rifugio Treviso	Passo Cereda	4hr 30	9km	1100m/1370m	2–3
11	Passo Cereda	Rifugio Boz	7hr 15	14km	1060m/700m	3+
12	Rifugio Boz	Rifugio Dal Piaz	6hr	15km	870m/600m	3
13	Rifugio Dal Piaz	Croce d'Aune	1hr 30	6km	–/980m	2

LISTING OF CICERONE GUIDES

BRITISH ISLES CHALLENGES, COLLECTIONS AND ACTIVITIES

The End to End Trail
The Mountains of England and Wales
　1 Wales
　2 England
The National Trails
The Relative Hills of Britain
The Ridges of England, Wales and Ireland
The UK Trailwalker's Handbook
Three Peaks, Ten Tors

MOUNTAIN LITERATURE

Unjustifiable Risk?

UK CYCLING

Border Country Cycle Routes
Lands End to John O'Groats Cycle Guide
Rural Rides
　2 East Surrey
South Lakeland Cycle Rides
The Lancashire Cycleway

SCOTLAND

Backpacker's Britain
　Central and Southern Scottish Highlands
Northern Scotland
Ben Nevis and Glen Coe
Border Pubs and Inns
North to the Cape
Not the West Highland Way
World Mountain Ranges: Scotland
Scotland's Best Small Mountains
Scotland's Far West
Scotland's Mountain Ridges
Scrambles in Lochaber
The Border Country
The Central Highlands
The Great Glen Way
The Isle of Skye
The Pentland Hills: A Walker's Guide
The Scottish Glens
　2 The Atholl Glens
　3 The Glens of Rannoch
　4 The Glens of Trossach
　5 The Glens of Argyll
　6 The Great Glen
The Southern Upland Way
The Speyside Way
The West Highland Way
Walking in Scotland's Far North
Walking in the Cairngorms
Walking in the Hebrides
Walking in the Ochils, Campsie Fells and Lomond Hills
Walking in Torridon
Walking Loch Lomond and the Trossachs
Walking on Harris and Lewis
Walking on Jura, Islay and Colonsay
Walking on the Isle of Arran
Walking on the Orkney and Shetland Isles
Walking the Galloway Hills
Walking the Lowther Hills
Walking the Munros
　1 Southern, Central and Western Highlands
　2 Northern Highlands and the Cairngorms
Winter Climbs Ben Nevis and Glen Coe
Winter Climbs in the Cairngorms

NORTHERN ENGLAND TRAILS

A Northern Coast to Coast Walk
Backpacker's Britain
　Northern England
Hadrian's Wall Path
The Dales Way
The Pennine Way
The Spirit of Hadrian's Wall

NORTH EAST ENGLAND, YORKSHIRE DALES AND PENNINES

A Canoeist's Guide to the North East
Historic Walks in North Yorkshire
South Pennine Walks
The Cleveland Way and the Yorkshire Wolds Way
The North York Moors
The Reivers Way
The Teesdale Way
The Yorkshire Dales Angler's Guide
The Yorkshire Dales
　North and East
　South and West
Walking in County Durham
Walking in Northumberland
Walking in the North Pennines
Walking in the Wolds
Walks in Dales Country
Walks in the Yorkshire Dales
Walks on the North York Moors
　Books 1 & 2

NORTH WEST ENGLAND AND THE ISLE OF MAN

A Walker's Guide to the Lancaster Canal
Historic Walks in Cheshire
Isle of Man Coastal Path
The Isle of Man
The Ribble Way
Walking in Lancashire
Walking in the Forest of Bowland and Pendle
Walking on the West Pennine Moors
Walks in Lancashire Witch Country
Walks in Ribble Country
Walks in Silverdale and Arnside
Walks in the Forest of Bowland

LAKE DISTRICT

An Atlas of the English Lakes
Coniston Copper Mines
Great Mountain Days in the Lake District
Lake District Winter Climbs
Roads and Tracks of the Lake District
Rocky Rambler's Wild Walks
Scrambles in the Lake District
　North & South
Short Walks in Lakeland
　1 South Lakeland
　2 North Lakeland
　3 West Lakeland
The Central Fells
The Cumbria Coastal Way
The Cumbria Way and the Allerdale Ramble
The Lake District Anglers' Guide
The Mid-Western Fells
The Near Eastern Fells

The Southern Fells
The Tarns of Lakeland
  1 West
  2 East
Tour of the Lake District

DERBYSHIRE, PEAK DISTRICT AND MIDLANDS
High Peak Walks
The Star Family Walks
Walking in Derbyshire
White Peak Walks
  The Northern Dales
  The Southern Dales

SOUTHERN ENGLAND
A Walker's Guide to the Isle of Wight
London – The definitive walking Guide
The Cotswold Way
The Greater Ridgeway
The Lea Valley Walk
The North Downs Way
The South Downs Way
The South West Coast Path
The Thames Path
Walking in Bedfordshire
Walking in Berkshire
Walking in Buckinghamshire
Walking in Kent
Walking in Sussex
Walking in the Isles of Scilly
Walking in the Thames Valley
Walking on Dartmoor

WALES AND WELSH BORDERS
Backpacker's Britain
  Wales
Glyndwr's Way
Great Mountain Days in Snowdonia
Hillwalking in Snowdonia
Hillwalking in Wales
  Vols 1 & 2
Offa's Dyke Path
Ridges of Snowdonia
Scrambles in Snowdonia
The Ascent of Snowdon
The Lleyn Peninsula Coastal Path
The Pembrokeshire Coastal Path
The Shropshire Hills
The Spirit Paths of Wales
Walking in Pembrokeshire

Walking on the Brecon Beacons
Welsh Winter Climbs

INTERNATIONAL CHALLENGES, COLLECTIONS AND ACTIVITIES
Canyoning
Europe's High Points

EUROPEAN CYCLING
Cycle Touring in France
Cycle Touring in Ireland
Cycle Touring in Spain
Cycle Touring in Switzerland
Cycling in the French Alps
Cycling the Canal du Midi
Cycling the River Loire
The Danube Cycleway
The Grand Traverse of the Massif Central
The Way of St James

AFRICA
Climbing in the Moroccan Anti-Atlas
Kilimanjaro: A Complete Trekker's Guide
Trekking in the Atlas Mountains
Walking in the Drakensberg

ALPS – CROSS-BORDER ROUTES
100 Hut Walks in the Alps
Across the Eastern Alps: E5
Alpine Points of View
Alpine Ski Mountaineering
  1 Western Alps
  2 Central and Eastern Alps
Chamonix to Zermatt Snowshoeing
Tour of Mont Blanc
Tour of Monte Rosa
Tour of the Matterhorn
Walking in the Alps
Walks and Treks in the Maritime Alps

PYRENEES AND FRANCE/SPAIN CROSS-BORDER ROUTES
Rock Climbs In The Pyrenees
The GR10 Trail
The Mountains of Andorra
The Pyrenean Haute Route
The Pyrenees

The Way of St James
  France
  Spain
Through the Spanish Pyrenees: GR11
Walks and Climbs in the Pyrenees

AUSTRIA
Klettersteig – Scrambles in the Northern Limestone Alps
Trekking in Austria's Hohe Tauern
Trekking in the Stubai Alps
Trekking in the Zillertal Alps
Walking in Austria

EASTERN EUROPE
The High Tatras
The Mountains of Romania
Walking in Bulgaria's National Parks
Walking in Hungary

FRANCE
Ecrins National Park
GR20: Corsica
Mont Blanc Walks
The Cathar Way
The GR5 Trail
The Robert Louis Stevenson Trail
Tour of the Oisans: The GR54
Tour of the Queyras
Tour of the Vanoise
Trekking in the Vosges and Jura
Vanoise Ski Touring
Walking in Provence
Walking in the Cathar Region
Walking in the Cevennes
Walking in the Dordogne
Walking in the Haute Savoie
  North
  South
Walking in the Languedoc
Walking in the Tarentaise and Beaufortain Alps
Walking on Corsica
Walking the French Gorges
Walks in Volcano Country

GERMANY
Germany's Romantic Road
King Ludwig Way
Walking in the Bavarian Alps

Walking in the Harz Mountains
Walking in the Salzkammergut
Walking the River Rhine Trail

HIMALAYA

Annapurna: A Trekker's Guide
Bhutan
Everest: A Trekker's Guide
Garhwal and Kumaon: A Trekker's and Visitor's Guide
Kangchenjunga: A Trekker's Guide
Langtang with Gosainkund and Helambu: A Trekker's Guide
Manaslu: A Trekker's Guide
The Mount Kailash Trek

IRELAND

Irish Coastal Walks
The Irish Coast to Coast Walk
The Mountains of Ireland

ITALY

Central Apennines of Italy
Gran Paradiso
Italian Rock
Italy's Sibillini National Park
Shorter Walks in the Dolomites
Through the Italian Alps
Trekking in the Apennines
Treks in the Dolomites
Via Ferratas of the Italian Dolomites Vols 1 & 2
Walking in Sicily
Walking in the Central Italian Alps
Walking in the Dolomites
Walking in Tuscany
Walking on the Amalfi Coast

MEDITERRANEAN

Jordan – Walks, Treks, Caves, Climbs and Canyons
The Ala Dag
The High Mountains of Crete
The Mountains of Greece
Treks and Climbs in Wadi Rum, Jordan
Walking in Malta
Western Crete

NORTH AMERICA

British Columbia
The Grand Canyon
The John Muir Trail
The Pacific Crest Trail

SOUTH AMERICA

Aconcagua and the Southern Andes
Torres del Paine

SCANDINAVIA

Trekking in Greenland
Walking in Norway

SLOVENIA, CROATIA AND MONTENEGRO

The Julian Alps of Slovenia
The Mountains of Montenegro
Trekking in Slovenia
Walking in Croatia

SPAIN AND PORTUGAL

Costa Blanca Walks
 1 West
 2 East
Mountain Walking in Southern Catalunya
The Mountains of Central Spain
Trekking through Mallorca
Via de la Plata
Walking in Madeira
Walking in Mallorca
Walking in the Algarve
Walking in the Canary Islands 2 East
Walking in the Cordillera Cantabrica
Walking in the Sierra Nevada
Walking on La Gomera and El Hierro
Walking on La Palma
Walking the GR7 in Andalucia
Walks and Climbs in the Picos de Europa

SWITZERLAND

Alpine Pass Route
Central Switzerland
The Bernese Alps
Tour of the Jungfrau Region
Walking in the Valais
Walking in Ticino
Walks in the Engadine

TECHNIQUES

Indoor Climbing
Map and Compass
Mountain Weather
Moveable Feasts
Outdoor Photography
Rock Climbing
Snow and Ice Techniques
Sport Climbing
The Book of the Bivvy
The Hillwalker's Guide to Mountaineering
The Hillwalker's Manual

MINI GUIDES

Avalanche!
Navigating with a GPS
Navigation
Pocket First Aid and Wilderness Medicine
Snow

For full and up-to-date information on our ever-expanding list of guides, visit our website:
www.cicerone.co.uk.

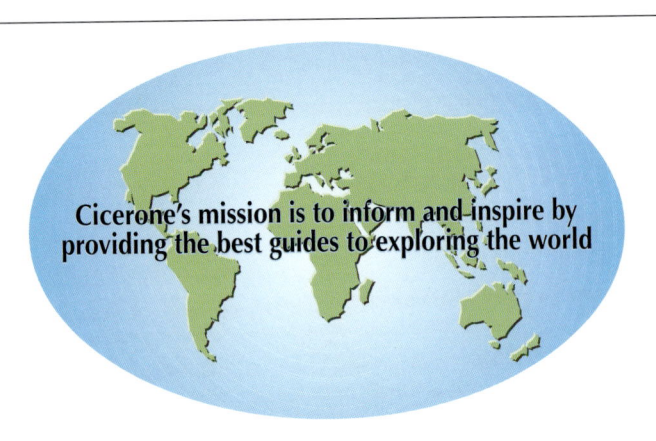

Cicerone's mission is to inform and inspire by providing the best guides to exploring the world

Since its foundation 40 years ago, Cicerone has specialised in publishing guidebooks and has built a reputation for quality and reliability. It now publishes nearly 300 guides to the major destinations for outdoor enthusiasts, including Europe, UK and the rest of the world.

Written by leading and committed specialists, Cicerone guides are recognised as the most authoritative. They are full of information, maps and illustrations so that the user can plan and complete a successful and safe trip or expedition – be it a long face climb, a walk over Lakeland fells, an alpine cycling tour, a Himalayan trek or a ramble in the countryside.

With a thorough introduction to assist planning, clear diagrams, maps and colour photographs to illustrate the terrain and route, and accurate and detailed text, Cicerone guides are designed for ease of use and access to the information.

If the facts on the ground change, or there is any aspect of a guide that you think we can improve, we are always delighted to hear from you.

Cicerone Press
2 Police Square Milnthorpe Cumbria LA7 7PY
Tel: 015395 62069 Fax: 015395 63417
info@cicerone.co.uk www.cicerone.co.uk

CICERONE